Italian Cooking

HALLIE DONNELLY
JANET KESSEL FLETCHER
Writers

SALLY W. SMITH
Editor

KEVIN SANCHEZ
Photographer

SUSAN MASSEY-WEIL
Food Stylist

LIZ ROSS
Photographic Stylist

CALIFORNIA
CULINARY
ACADEMY

Hallie Donnelly (left), a native San Franciscan, has been a chef-caterer for ten years. She holds a degree in music from the University of California, Berkeley, and attended the California Culinary Academy. In France, she studied cooking with Michel Guérard, Roger Vergé, and André Daguin. The author of a book on sushi and sashimi, she has had her own cooking school and television show. She is presently executive chef of the Scottsdale Culinary Institute, a training program for food-industry professionals, and also a consultant for hotels and restaurants. **Janet Kessel Fletcher** (right) is a free-lance food and wine writer and editor. She holds a degree in economics from Stanford University and attended the Culinary Institute of America in Hyde Park, N.Y. She has cooked in several west-coast restaurants, including the highly acclaimed Chez Panisse, and now writes a weekly restaurant column for the Oakland *Tribune*. In addition, she writes and produces newsletters, brochures, and promotional literature for clients in the food and wine industry. Ms. Donnelly and Ms. Fletcher are the co-authors of the California Culinary Academy book *Appetizers and Hors d'Oeuvres*.

The California Culinary Academy In the forefront of American institutions leading the culinary renaissance in this country, the California Culinary Academy in San Francisco has gained a reputation as one of the most outstanding professional chef training schools in the world. With a teaching staff recruited from the best restaurants of Western Europe, the Academy educates students from around the world in the preparation of classical cuisine. The recipes in this book were created in consultation with the chefs of the Academy. For information about the Academy, write the Office of the Dean, California Culinary Academy, 625 Polk Street, San Francisco, CA 94102.

Front Cover
Ravioli with a filling of escarole and two cheeses (see page 42) sauced with a hearty Sugo di Pomodoro (see page 36) makes a thoroughly Italian main course. In Italian style, follow it with a simple salad of mixed greens (see Insalata Mista, page 100).

Title Page
Italian cooking is a flavorful gathering of regional specialties. Throughout Italy, however, good wine and bread are appreciated.

Back Cover
Upper Left: Leeks, carrots, onions, garlic, and herbs are just some of the ingredients that go into a rich veal stock.
Upper Right: A mixture of red, green, and yellow bell peppers, slowly cooked with tomatoes, herbs, and garlic, makes a colorful appetizer (Peperonata, page 13).
Lower Left: For a luscious dessert, try a cheesecake, rich with raisins, pine nuts, and chocolate (see Torta di Ricotta, page 114), accompanied with a glass of sweet wine.
Lower Right: Trout garnished with lemon and parsley enter the fish poacher.

Special Thanks to Biordi Art Imports; Luciano Creations, supplied by Shears & Window Garden Court; Jeffrey Thomas Fine & Rare Books; Ceramic Showcase; Forrest Jones; Molinari Delicatessen; Debbie Slutsky; Susan White (all San Francisco); Ed and Kaycey Garrone, Monterey, Calif.; David Beckwith, Carmel, Calif.; Derna Passalacqua, Tempe, Ariz.; Maria Zacco, Rome, Italy.

Contributors
Calligraphers
Keith Carlson, Chuck Wertman

Illustrator
Edith Allgood

Additional Photographers
Laurie Black, CCA chefs, below left; Alan Copeland, at the Academy; Marshall Gordon, pages 14, 16, 38, 43, 67, and 80; Kit Morris, authors, at left; Michael Lamotte, back cover, upper left and lower right; Jackson Vereen, page 66

Additional Food Stylists
M. Susan Broussard, page 66; Amy Nathan, back cover, upper left and lower right; Doug Warne, pages 14, 16, 38, 43, 67, and 80

Copy Chief
Melinda E. Levine

Editorial Coordinator
Kate Rider

Copyeditor
Antonio Padial

Proofreader
Andrea Y. Connolly

Indexer
Elinor Lindheimer

Editorial Assistants
Tamara Mallory, Raymond F. Quinton, Leslie Tilley

Composition and Pagination by
Linda M. Bouchard, Bob Miller

Series format designed by
Linda Hinrichs, Carol Kramer

Production by
Studio 165

Separations by
Color Tech Corp.

Lithographed in U.S.A. by
Webcrafters, Inc.

The California Culinary Academy series is produced by the staff of Ortho Information Services.

Publisher
Robert J. Dolezal

Production Director
Ernie S. Tasaki

Series Managing Editor
Sally W. Smith

Systems Manager
Leonard D. Grotta

Address all inquiries to
Ortho Information Services
575 Market Street
San Francisco, CA 94105

Chevron Chemical Company
575 Market Street, San Francisco, CA 94105

CONTENTS

Italian Cooking

Like any great cuisine, Italian cooking starts with fresh, local ingredients. Just as outstanding grapes make a fine wine, the best basics become delectable meals.

Introduction to Italian Cooking

Tomatoes and garlic. Fresh fish and fresh herbs. Hot pasta and vibrant green pesto. These are just some of the many flavors and colors of the lively Italian table. In the following chapters you'll find specialties from every region and corner of Italy, including traditional dishes from fine home cooks and recipes that have made restaurants famous. This first chapter introduces Italian cooking region by region. It also features an explanation of the typical Italian meal and a guide to the ingredients that characterize authentic Italian food. *Buon appetito!*

THE ITALIAN TABLE, REGION BY REGION

Italian cooking is primarily a collection of regional cuisines derived from local ingredients, climate, and geography. The recipes in this book, which are identified by place of origin, are drawn from every corner of Italy.

To appreciate the diversity of Italian cooking, take a closer look at its specialties region by region. From north to south:

Piedmont is wine country, source of some of the best wines of Italy. Barolo, Barbaresco, Nebbiolo d'Alba, Dolcetto, and the sparkling Asti Spumante are among the Piedmontese wines enjoyed worldwide. The region is also renowned for its rare white truffles, for the slender breadsticks of Turin, and for the pungent anchovy-garlic dip, Bagna Cauda (see page 19).

The Valle d'Aosta is a mountainous region known for game and for the rich, nutty fontina cheese. The mountain dwellers of the Valle d'Aosta are big consumers of Polenta (see page 58), potatoes, and bread, all of which are frequently layered with or dipped in melted fontina.

Lombardy is also polenta country. Milan, the urban center of the region, is famous for its cooking—for example, Risotto alla Milanese (see page 61) and a dish of braised veal shanks called Osso Buco (see page 77).

Trentino–Alto Adige features a Germanic style of cooking, not surprising given its proximity to Austria and Switzerland. Fresh pork, smoked pork, and sausages are popular here and may be served with German-style sauerkraut. Many dishes would be equally at home on a German or Austrian table; apple strudel, for example, is a common local dessert. Even some of the white wines of the region are made in the German or Alsatian style.

The Friuli–Venezia Giulia region is not well known for its food, although the ham of San Daniele is highly regarded. The white wines of Friuli, however—especially the Tocai, Pinot Bianco, and Pinot Grigio—are exported to the United States and are delicious with ham and seafood.

The Veneto includes Venice, with its famous scampi from the nearby gulf (see Gamberi del Veneto, page 70), calves' liver with onions, Risi e Bisi (see page 61), and exquisite fish soups. Soave, perhaps the most popular Italian white wine in America, comes from the Veneto.

Emilia-Romagna has a world-renowned cuisine. It is rich, sophisticated cooking more dependent on butter and cream than on olive oil. Bologna produces wonderful sausages and cured meats like mortadella; Parma gives the world Parmesan and prosciutto; Modena produces the sweet-tart balsamic vinegar (*aceto balsamico*) that is increasingly imported to the United States. Bologna is also known for its fresh homemade pasta, used in an endless array of dishes such as *tagliatelle* with Ragù Bolognese (see page 36) and Tortellini in Brodo (see page 38).

Liguria is a coastal region known for its seafood, especially its mussels. Perhaps the most famous Ligurian dish, however, is the aromatic garlic-and-basil sauce called Pesto (see page 35). Tossed with hot pasta and potatoes (see page 41), pesto is a lively reminder of the warmth of the Ligurian sun.

Tuscany is the home of Chianti, of Bistecca alla Fiorentina (see page 76), and of rustic bean soups such as Pasta e Fagioli (see page 28). Tuscan olive oil is prized throughout the world, and its fruity character infuses almost all Tuscan fare. Some of the best cooking in Italy is found in the many *trattorie* (casual restaurants) of Florence and the Tuscan countryside.

The Umbria region is known for black truffles, for pork and pork sausage, and for Orvieto, a light white wine.

The Marches has a varied cuisine, from the *brodetto* (fish soup) of the coast to the *porchetta* (suckling pig) of the interior. It is not a cuisine well known outside its region.

Latium, also known as Lazio, is the region of Rome and is thus one of Italy's gastronomic centers. Roman cooks have given us Saltimbocca (see page 84), Fettuccine Carbonara (see page 41), Carciofi alla Romana (see page 110), and dozens of other popular dishes. Roman restaurants often feature suckling pig or suckling lamb roasted on a spit; vegetables are also served in abundance, from Piselli al Prosciutto (see page 108) to the assertive Cime di Rape alla Romana (see page 110).

Abruzzi is a mountainous region, its cooking hearty but unrefined. Fish, often in the form of Scapece (see page 14), dominates menus near the coast; inland, the diet revolves around pork, a broad variety of vegetables, and the local *scamorze* cheese.

The Campania region includes Naples and Sorrento and boasts a lovely coastline. The cuisine is heavily influenced by what comes from local waters, such as mussels, clams, and squid. The sunny climate yields tomatoes galore for use in salads, in pasta sauce, and on pizza. Neapolitan cooks are not known for their subtle touch; many dishes are aggressively seasoned with garlic, oregano, and olive oil. Pizza alle Vongole (see page 58) and Spaghetti con Aglio e Olio (see page 37) are typical of the assertive flavors of Neapolitan cooking. Among its other distinguishing features is dried pasta, which is much more common here than in the north; fresh pasta is rarely served. The world-renowned mozzarella and provolone cheeses are native to the region; they turn up on pizza, in Calzone (see page 55), and in tomato salads (see Insalata Capricciosa, page 100). Vegetables are used in abundance, especially eggplant, zucchini, spinach, and sweet peppers.

Apulia, in the "heel" of Italy, is surrounded by water. Naturally, the cooking is heavily dependent on seafood. Fish and shellfish fried in the local olive oil (Frutte di Mare Fritti, page 66) are a specialty of the province of Bari. The cooking is similar to that of Naples.

Basilicata is not a region with a strong culinary identity. It is a poor region agriculturally; olive oil is its main product. The cuisine is generally spicy and straightforward.

Calabria, at the tip of the Italian "boot," is also a poor region; its main crops are olives and citrus. The Calabrian diet is a modest one based on dried pasta, tomatoes, eggplant, peppers, and seafood.

Sicily is home to a fascinating array of dishes. The cooking has much in common with that of southern Italy: olive oil, dried pasta, tomatoes, eggplant, peppers, and seafood are used abundantly. Sicilian cooking, however, is more aggressively seasoned—often with hot red peppers. Many dishes, such as Caponatina (see page 23), have a sweet-and-sour component. Sicilians also have a noted sweet tooth, which they assuage with ices, ice cream, and such elaborate creations as Cassata Donna Lugata (see page 122).

A hand-cranked pasta machine makes light work of homemade pasta. Cut by hand or by machine to desired width as shown here (clockwise from left rear): lasagne (see page 42), pappardelle (see page 41) beside uncut dough—both made with Pasta Verde (see page 34), linguine (see page 90) made with Pasta di Herbe (see page 35), and fettuccine (see pages 40–41) made with Pasta di Pomodori (see page 35). Pasta is usually served as a "first course" following the antipasto and preceding the main dish (see page 8).

THE ITALIAN TABLE, COURSE BY COURSE

Whether formal or informal, the Italian meal follows a pattern that rarely varies. It isn't built around a main course, as in America; instead, it is a series of small courses, each of relatively equal weight.

In the typical progression, an Italian meal might begin with an *aperitivo* (see page 13), perhaps a glass of sweet or dry vermouth or a Campari and soda. In a private home, the host might offer olives or roasted almonds as an accompaniment.

The first course of an Italian meal is an antipasto, usually an assortment of cured meats, pickled or marinated vegetables, or marinated shellfish. Peperonata (see page 13) and sliced prosciutto, served together, make an appealing and typical antipasto.

Following the antipasto is the "first course" *(primo piatto)*. It may be a risotto, a soup, or a pasta dish. Tortellini in Brodo (see page 38) or Risotto al Limone (see page 61) are both typical first courses.

The second course *(secondo piatto)* may be fish, fowl, or meat. A pork roast seasoned with rosemary (Arrosto di Maiale con Rosmarino, page 84) or a roast chicken stuffed with *porcini* mushrooms (see page 88) would be an appropriate second course. With rare exceptions, vegetables, such as Cime di Rape alla Romana (see page 110) and Piselli al Prosciutto (see page 108), are not served on the same plate as the meat but are offered in separate side dishes.

A salad of raw or very simply cooked greens or vegetables, such as Insalata Mista (see page 100), may follow the second course. If the second course is a grill, the salad sometimes accompanies it in a separate dish; the Roman Insalata dell' Estate (see page 101) is an example.

Italians rarely end a meal with dessert. Instead, meals end with fresh fruit, fruit macerated in wine (Pesche al Vino, page 114), or a wedge of ripe cheese. Espresso, drunk black, is served after the fruit or cheese course; in a home, espresso is served away from the table.

Restaurant Cooking and Home Cooking

The dishes featured in the following chapters are drawn from a variety of sources. Some, such as Pollo con Cavolo al Limone (see page 88), are representative of Italian home cooking and are rarely found in restaurants outside of small, family-run *trattorie*.

Other dishes in this book are rarely made outside of restaurants, although there is no reason they can't be duplicated in the home. Carpaccio (see page 19) is closely associated with Harry's Bar in Venice, where it was invented. Today many restaurants offer it, but the home cook can also prepare it with ease.

In Italy, pizza, bread, and ice cream are rarely made at home. Pizza is a snack food, bought by the slice. Ice cream and fruit ices are enjoyed in caffès or bought from street vendors. Fresh bread is purchased daily from a bakery.

Many American cooks, however, delight in making these items, so the following chapters include recipes for pizza and calzone, traditional breads, and seasonal ice creams.

A LITTLE CULINARY GRAMMAR

For those unfamiliar with Italian, a few tips may help in understanding the terms in this book.

Italian nouns are either masculine *(il pomodoro)* or feminine *(la pera)*. The plural is formed by changing the ending of the word. The preceding articles agree with the nouns.

Examples: *il pomodoro* (the tomato), *i pomodori* (the tomatoes); *la pera* (the pear), *le pere* (the pears); *l'insalata* (the salad), *le insalate* (the salads); *l'antipasto* (the antipasto), *gli antipasti* (the antipastos).

Adjectives, which usually follow nouns, generally agree with the nouns that they modify. Thus: *calamari verdi* (green squid) but *lasagne verde* (green lasagne), *fritto misto* (mixed fry) but *insalata mista* (mixed salad).

These are very general guidelines; for almost every rule there is an exception.

THE ITALIAN KITCHEN IN AMERICA

To reproduce the authentic flavors of the Italian kitchen, stock your pantry and refrigerator with some of the items that Italians use repeatedly. Many of these foods are available in well-supplied supermarkets. If you have difficulty finding them, check specialty stores, Italian markets, and mail-order sources.

Amaretti are crisp almond macaroons sprinkled with coarse sugar. Amaretti are delicious with after-dinner espresso; they can be crumbled and sprinkled over sugared peaches or ice cream sundaes or folded into sweetened whipped cream to make the frozen Biscuit Tortoni (see page 120).

Anchovies are generally available in supermarkets as oil-packed fillets. Far superior are the whole salt-packed anchovies available in some Italian markets and specialty stores. To use whole anchovies, rinse off the salt. Under cold running water, split them open lengthwise with your fingers and lift away the skeleton. Anchovies add a pungent salted-fish flavor to sauces, butters, dressings, pizza, and stuffings.

Arborio rice is the stubby, short-grain polished rice grown in Italy's Po Valley. Its particular starch composition makes it the preferred rice for Italian risotto (see page 61). Italian markets, specialty stores, and some well-stocked supermarkets offer Arborio rice.

Arugula, also known as rocket or roquette, is a salad green that is increasingly cultivated in this country. When young, it has a mild nutty flavor; older leaves develop a peppery pungency. Use young arugula leaves in mixed green salads (Insalata Mista, page 100) or toss them at the last minute with hot pasta. To store arugula, wash and dry, then wrap in paper towels and place in a plastic bag; it will keep in the refrigerator for two to three days.

Balsamic vinegar is an aromatic sweet/tart wood-aged vinegar made from Italian red wine. The best balsamic vinegar is aged for many years and can be very expensive. However, less expensive bottlings are now widely available in this country. The vinegar imparts a distinctive mellow flavor to salads, vegetable dishes, and sauces (see Roasted Balsamic Onions, page 22, and Balsamic Vinaigrette, page 99).

Capers are the unopened buds of a Mediterranean bush; they are generally packed in brine but may occasionally be found packed in salt. Capers add a piquant note to countless Italian dishes, from Agnello con Acciughe e Caperi (see page 82) to Caponatina (see page 23). Choose the tiny nonpareil type rather than the large capers.

Ceci are also known as chick-peas or garbanzo beans. They are widely available canned in supermarkets; some health-food stores and specialty markets carry dried ceci, too. Marinated ceci are often served in Italy as part of an antipasto platter, with sliced meats; they are also added to hearty soups containing vegetables and pasta or rice (see Minestrone Primavera, page 28).

Grappa is a strong, clear Italian brandy made from the distilled remains of pressed grapes. In many Italian homes and restaurants, it is offered after dinner as a digestive.

Italian parsley is a flat-leaf parsley, as opposed to the curly-leaf parsley common in American supermarkets. It has a more pungent flavor and is preferred for Italian cooking. It is fairly widely available; it is also easy to cultivate at home.

Olives are an important ingredient in Italian cooking. They may be served before the meal with an *aperitivo* or as part of a platter of *antipasti* (see Italian Olives, page 15). Olives also impart their pungent flavor to sautéed dishes. For Italian cooking, use imported Mediterranean olives. Among Italian varieties available in specialty markets are the Lugano (a brine-cured, purple-black olive), the Ponentine (a brine-cured, purple-black olive, milder than the Lugano), and the Gaeta (a salt-cured, wrinkled black olive rubbed with oil). French, Greek, or Moroccan varieties are satisfactory substitutes.

Polenta is coarsely ground yellow cornmeal used in a variety of northern Italian dishes (see pages 58–59). Many supermarkets sell polenta; health-food stores and Italian markets often carry it in bulk. It should be stored in a cool, dry place and used within six months.

Porcini are the same wild mushrooms known as *cèpes* in French and as *boletus edulis* in Latin. Fresh *porcini* are fleshy, velvety, and earthy in flavor; the dried porcini are highly aromatic, with an intense woodsy flavor. The recipes in this book call for dried porcini, which are available in Italian markets and specialty stores; they are expensive, but a little goes a long way. To reconstitute, soak them until softened in warm water, about one hour. Lift them out of the soaking liquid with a slotted spoon, strain the liquid through cheesecloth to remove any grit, and save liquid for soups and sauces. Store unused dried porcini in an airtight container in a cool, dry place.

Salt cod is a popular food in southern Italy, even when fresh cod is available. It has a firm, meaty texture that can stand up to hearty treatments (see Baccalà Fritto alla Siciliana, page 44). Salt cod is sold in Italian markets in long slabs; supermarkets occasionally sell it packed in wooden boxes. It must be soaked first in several changes of cold water for about a day to soften it and remove much of the salt. Before soaking, it will keep indefinitely in a cool, dry place.

Semolina is an ivory-colored flour ground from high-protein durum wheat. It is available in both coarse and fine grinds. Semolina is used in most factory-made dried pasta because it makes a sturdy dough that stands up to the kneading and molding. Semolina is also used to make the dumplings known as *gnocchi* (see page 61) and is used in some Italian breads and puddings.

Fresh and canned tomatoes are among the most widely used ingredients in Italian cooking, especially southern Italian cooking. The pear-shaped plum tomatoes are preferred for sauces, as they have a high proportion of meat to seeds and juice. Use fresh plum tomatoes only when they are ripe and fragrant; otherwise, canned plum tomatoes are a better choice. The imported Italian plum tomatoes are generally packed riper than American brands and are preferable.

Sun-dried tomatoes are sometimes available in cellophane packets but are more usually packed in olive oil, which is the form called for in the recipes in this book. Gourmet shops and well-stocked supermarkets carry them. They have a sweet, almost candied tomato flavor and a chewy texture. They are also sometimes extremely salty and should be used in small quantities, to garnish pizza, to flavor pasta dough (see Pasta di Pomodori, page 35), to give a lift to a salad (see Fagioli Bianchi con Peperonata, page 100), or to intensify the flavor of a tomato sauce. Store sun-dried tomatoes, covered with oil, in a capped jar in the refrigerator. They will keep for an indefinite period.

Tomato paste is used to add a concentrated tomato flavor to sauces and stews. Store leftover tomato paste in a nonmetal container covered with a thin film of olive oil; it will keep in the refrigerator for up to two weeks or in the freezer indefinitely. Alternatively, some markets now sell imported Italian tomato paste in tubes, allowing you to use as little as you need and refrigerate the rest indefinitely.

To begin a meal Italians offer
savory antipasti such as cured
meats, olives, some of the
country's famed cheeses, or
giardiniera—pickled vegetables.

Antipasti

An Italian meal usually begins with an antipasto, an appetizer course. In this chapter you'll find a representative assortment of antipasti, from the bread-based *crostini* (see page 17) and vegetables with dips (see Legumi in Pinzimonio, page 23) to elegant Carpaccio (see page 19). The chapter also contains an explanation of the Italian before-dinner *aperitivo* (see page 13), step-by-step photographs showing how to roast red peppers (see page 14) and prepare artichoke hearts (see page 16), special features on Italian wines (page 17) and cheeses (page 20), and a description of the tempting cured meats and sausages of Italy (see page 23).

Mixed sweet peppers make tricolored Peperonata, a lively late-summer antipasto. For a more substantial first course, pair the peppers with sliced mozzarella.

ANTIPASTI

The word *antipasto* literally means "before the pasta" and historically refers to any dish served before the pasta course. In actuality, however, even a meal without a pasta course can be launched with a tempting selection of *antipasti*. The portions should be small and the flavors piquant to stimulate the appetite. Popular antipasti include marinated vegetables like Peperonata (see opposite page); marinated fish such as Insalata di Calamari (see page 14) or Scapece (see page 14); thin-sliced salty cheeses and hams, such as Ricotta Salata e Prosciutto (see page 21); olives, marinated or plain; and rustic grilled garlic breads like Bruschetta (opposite page).

ANTIPASTI GRATINATI
Broiled fontina fingers

Fontina melts and browns beautifully over baked eggplant spears in this easy Bolognese appetizer.

    4 Japanese eggplants
    ¼ cup olive oil
    ½ pound fontina cheese
       Salt and freshly ground
       black pepper
    ¼ cup minced Italian parsley

1. Preheat oven to 400° F. Trim ends off eggplants and slice each lengthwise into four "fingers," approximately ¼ inch thick. Brush a baking sheet with 2 tablespoons of the olive oil. Place eggplant slices on sheet and brush with remaining oil. Bake slices until brown (about 12 to 15 minutes). Transfer to paper towels.

2. Preheat broiler 5 minutes. Slice cheese ¼ inch thick and place a slice on each "finger." Put cheese-topped eggplant slices in broiler and brown, watching carefully, until cheese is bubbly. Transfer to a serving platter or individual plates; sprinkle with salt, pepper, and parsley.

Makes 16 fingers, or 8 individual servings.

BRUSCHETTA
Grilled Tuscan garlic bread

Nothing proves the Italians' love of simple food so well as their fondness for *bruschetta*, the Italian version of garlic toast. Made from sturdy country bread grilled (ideally over an open fire), then liberally rubbed with garlic and brushed with the new-crop olive oil, it is an earthy invention, direct and utterly delicious. Because it is so simple, it requires the best olive oil. Serve Bruschetta by itself with a young red wine, or add a platter of olives, prosciutto, and Parmesan. Note that the oil-and-garlic mixture should sit for at least several hours or as long as three days. The longer the oil sits, the better and stronger the garlic flavor. If you're going to keep it more than a few hours, store cooled oil in a covered jar in a cool place.

> 16 slices coarse country-style bread, ⅓ inch thick
> ¾ cup olive oil
> 3 tablespoons minced garlic
> Coarse salt and freshly ground black pepper

1. Heat olive oil and garlic in a saucepan until a light haze forms. Garlic should not be allowed to brown. Let oil sit for several days, if possible, or at least a few hours.

2. Preheat broiler 5 minutes. Toast bread on both sides until golden (or, even better, toast it over an open fire). Gently reheat garlic-oil mixture. Brush it generously on one side of each bread slice. Sprinkle slices with salt and pepper and serve hot.

Makes 16 pieces.

PEPERONATA
Mixed marinated peppers

Sweet peppers stewed slowly with tomatoes, herbs, and garlic are a popular summer first course in southern Italy. Serve them with crusty bread to mop up the aromatic juices, or offer Peperonata as part of a larger antipasto platter along with Bruschetta (at left), sliced prosciutto, black olives, and a little Insalata di Calamari (see page 14). Select meaty peppers that feel heavy for their size.

> ½ cup olive oil
> 2 tablespoons minced garlic
> ½ yellow onion, minced
> 2 red bell peppers
> 2 green bell peppers
> 1 yellow bell pepper (if unavailable, substitute another red or green pepper)
> 2 tomatoes, peeled, seeded, and coarsely chopped (see page 29)
> 2 teaspoons salt
> ¼ cup fresh oregano leaves
> ½ red onion, in paper-thin slices, for garnish
> 2 tablespoons minced parsley, for garnish
> 2 tablespoons fruity olive oil (optional)

1. In a large skillet over medium heat, heat the ½ cup olive oil until it is hot but not smoking. Add garlic and onion and sauté, stirring until lightly colored (about 3 minutes).

2. Halve peppers; remove seeds and trim away white ribs. Cut lengthwise into strips ½ inch wide. Add all peppers to skillet at one time and stir to blend with garlic-onion mixture. Add tomatoes and salt and mix gently. Place oregano leaves on top. Cover and simmer slowly until peppers are soft (about 12 to 15 minutes). Remove from heat and transfer to serving bowl to cool.

3. Serve peppers at room temperature, garnishing the top with the sliced red onion and minced parsley. If desired, drizzle with the 2 tablespoons fruity olive oil just before serving.

Makes about 3½ cups, or enough for 8 people as part of an antipasto platter.

THE ITALIAN APERITIVO

Whether served at home, in a caffè, or in a formal restaurant, an Italian meal is generally preceded by an *aperitivo*—a beverage designed to awaken the palate and perk up the appetite. For an aperitivo, most Italians prefer the wine-based blends to high-alcohol spirits such as whiskey and gin. Most Italian aperitivi are faintly or even frankly bitter, the better to pique the appetite. Among the most popular:

Bitters are made from the bitter and aromatic essences of plants, seeds, roots, flowers, leaves, bark, stems, and fruits dissolved in an alcohol base. The best known brand of the bitters is Campari. As with most such concoctions, its exact formula is a highly guarded secret. Bitters are almost always mixed with soda; in fact, premixed and bottled Campari-and-soda is widely available. Fernet Branca and Amer Picon are other brands of Italian bitters.

Cynar is a wine-based aperitivo flavored with artichoke. Serve it as you would vermouth.

Vermouth is made from wine that has been flavored with roots, herbs, seeds, or other aromatics and given a bitter edge with quinine, then fortified with brandy, sweetened with sugar, and possibly colored with caramel. Cinzano, Martini & Rossi, and Punt e Mes are all manufacturers of sweet Italian vermouth; each employs a slightly different formula. Serve Italian vermouth well chilled, either neat, on the rocks, or with a splash of soda and twist of lemon.

In addition, more Italian producers are making dry sparkling wine by the Champagne method. Some of the best of these are exported to the United States. Look for Prosecco and Ferrari, among others. These dry sparklers make excellent apéritifs.

HOW TO ROAST RED PEPPERS

1. Hold peppers over an open gas flame or charcoal fire, or place them under a broiler. Turn often until blackened on all sides. Transfer peppers to a paper bag; close and set aside until cool (15 to 20 minutes).

2. Peel peppers; halve; remove stem and seeds. Lay halves flat and use dull side of a small knife to scrape away any black bits of skin and stray seeds. Slice into ¼-inch strips.

Roasted Red Peppers Prepare 2 red bell peppers as directed above. Put sliced peppers in a medium bowl; add 1 clove finely minced garlic, 2 tablespoons extravirgin olive oil, and 1 teaspoon minced fresh oregano. Salt to taste. Toss to blend and let marinate at room temperature for 1 hour before using.

INSALATA DI CALAMARI
Squid salad

Squid are found in abundance all along Italy's lengthy coastline. Because they're so plentiful and inexpensive, they're made into countless different dishes. Southern Italians turn squid into cool, refreshing salads, seasoning them with garlic, hot peppers, and vinegar, then adding sweet peppers and two kinds of onions for color and crunch.

> 2½ pounds squid
>   Salt
> ½ red onion, thinly sliced
> 1 green bell pepper, seeded, ribs removed, and sliced in matchsticks
> 1 red bell pepper, seeded, ribs removed, and sliced in matchsticks
> 1 bunch green onions, sliced in half lengthwise, then in 1-inch lengths on the bias
> 2 small carrots, peeled and cut in matchsticks
> ¾ cup olive oil
> 7 tablespoons white wine vinegar
> 1 tablespoon lemon juice
> ½ teaspoon each *dried basil, oregano, and thyme*
> ½ teaspoon freshly ground black pepper
> 1 teaspoon minced garlic
> 1 dash hot sauce or *pinch hot red-pepper flakes*
> 1 tablespoon balsamic vinegar
> 2 dashes Worcestershire sauce

1. Clean squid and slice bodies into ½-inch rings (see page 66). Poach rings and tentacles in plenty of salted water at a low boil just until they turn white (about ½ to 1 minute). Drain; quickly transfer to a bowl of ice water to stop the cooking. When completely cool, drain well and pat dry.

2. In a large bowl combine squid, onions, peppers, green onions, and carrots.

3. In a bowl whisk together olive oil, wine vinegar, lemon juice, dried herbs, pepper, garlic, hot sauce, balsamic vinegar, and Worcestershire sauce. Add salt to taste. Pour over squid and vegetables; taste and adjust seasoning as necessary. Chill at least 30 minutes.

Serves 8 to 10.

Make-Ahead Tip The salad may be made up to 2 days ahead and stored, tightly covered, in the refrigerator. Taste and adjust seasoning before serving.

SCAPECE
Marinated whole fish

Like the Latin American *escabeche*, fish prepared *a scapece* is first floured, then fried, then marinated and served cool. It makes a pretty and piquant first course, surrounded with greens, if desired, or with assorted black and green olives. A crisp and simple white wine—an Italian Verdicchio, for example, or a California Sauvignon Blanc—would be fitting with this Abruzzese appetizer.

> 4 small whole white fish, about 1 pound each, with head and tail intact.
>   Flour seasoned with salt and pepper, for dredging
> 1 cup olive oil
> ½ cup coarsely chopped onion
> 1½ cups white wine
> ¼ cup lemon juice
> 1½ teaspoons freshly ground black pepper
> 1 teaspoon minced fresh lemon thyme (optional)
> 3 tablespoons grated lemon rind mixed with 3 tablespoons minced parsley
>   Lemon wedges, for garnish

1. Clean and scale fish (or have fish merchant do it). Dredge fish in seasoned flour, shaking off excess. Heat oil in a large skillet until a haze forms; do not allow oil to smoke. Fry fish on both sides until well browned (about 5 minutes per side). Transfer fish with a slotted spatula to a glass or enamel dish.

2. In same skillet over medium heat, sauté onions until slightly softened, about 3 minutes. Add wine, 1 tablespoon of the lemon juice, pepper, and lemon thyme (if used). Boil mixture 1 minute, then remove from heat. Cool 2 minutes, then pour over fish. Add remaining lemon juice and half the lemon rind–parsley mixture. Marinate at least 3 hours or up to 1 day. (If you are marinating fish longer than 3 hours, refrigerate it; remove from refrigerator 1 hour before serving.)

3. To serve, lift fish out of marinade and place on serving platter. If desired, fillet fish before serving and arrange fillets on the platter. Garnish fish with remaining lemon rind–parsley mixture and surround with lemon wedges.

Serves 8.

ITALIAN OLIVES

Personalize storebought olives in your own garlicky marinade. Serve them with the makings of little open-faced Italian "sandwiches": good bread, sliced Parmesan or fontina, and a cruet of fruity olive oil.

- 1 quart cracked black olives in brine
- ½ cup olive oil
- 7 cloves garlic, peeled and left whole
- 2 cups red wine vinegar
- 2 tablespoons black peppercorns
- 2 roasted red peppers (see opposite page), julienned
- 1 cup coarsely chopped fresh fennel
  Salt, to taste

Drain olives, pat dry, and coat lightly with olive oil. In a medium-sized pot combine garlic, vinegar, and peppercorns. Bring to a boil, remove from heat, and cool slightly. Pour over olives. Add peppers and fennel; marinate at room temperature at least 2 hours. Season to taste with salt before serving. Olives keep indefinitely if refrigerated in a clean glass jar.

Serves 6 generously.

Small fried fish soak up a cool lemon marinade in Scapece, a flavorful first course for a warm evening.

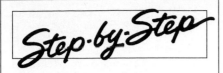

PREPARING BABY ARTICHOKE HEARTS

When preparing baby artichoke hearts, choose artichokes no larger than 1½ inches in diameter. They should feel crisp and firm and have tightly closed leaves.

1. *Pull off dark green outer leaves to reveal the pale green heart.*

2. *Cut about ⅓ inch off top; trim stems. Rub all over with lemon or soak in acidulated water.*

To cook Prepare baby artichoke hearts as directed above. Place trimmed hearts in a saucepan with acidulated salted water to cover. Boil until just tender, about 5 minutes. Drain, pat thoroughly dry, and put in a clean bowl or jar. Cover completely with olive oil. Oil-covered hearts can be stored, covered, in refrigerator for up to a month.

LEGUMI AL SOTTO
Marinated autumn vegetables

You've heard of speaking *sotto voce* (underneath the voice). Vegetables prepared *al sotto* are "underneath" a marinade—here, an herb-scented blend of lemon, vinegar, and olive oil. The dish is a favorite throughout Italy, served with salami or *coppa* (see page 23) and with bread to soak up the juices. Make it a day or two ahead to allow the flavors to marry.

       1½ pounds mushrooms
        1 head cauliflower
        6 ribs celery
        ¼ cup fresh lemon juice
        ½ cup white wine vinegar
        5 cups water
        ¼ cup fresh oregano leaves
        ¼ cup fresh basil leaves
        1 teaspoon salt
        2 tablespoons dried lemon
           thyme or ¼ cup fresh lemon
           verbena leaves (optional)
        1 cup olive oil
           Salt and pepper
        ½ pound small, oil-cured
           black olives
           Additional minced basil and
           oregano, for garnish

1. Trim, clean, and quarter mushrooms. Break cauliflower into bite-sized florets. Trim celery into 3-inch lengths.

2. In a large saucepan combine lemon juice, vinegar, water, oregano, basil, salt, and lemon thyme (if used). Bring to a simmer and simmer gently 5 minutes. Add mushrooms and cook until just tender (about 5 minutes). With a slotted spoon transfer mushrooms to a bowl. Add cauliflower to liquid and cook until crisp-tender. With a slotted spoon, remove to the mushroom bowl.

3. Raise heat to high and reduce liquid to 1½ cups. Remove from heat, strain, and whisk in olive oil. (It may not emulsify completely.) Add salt and pepper to taste. Pour dressing over vegetables in bowl. Add celery and olives and allow to cool completely. Garnish with additional basil and oregano leaves.

Serves 8 generously.

FRITTATA DI CARCIOFI
Open-faced artichoke omelet

To call a frittata an "open-faced omelet" is just the start of a definition. A frittata is thicker than an omelet, for one thing, and it's often served barely warm. But like an omelet, it's the basis for a cook's own inspirations. Butter-steamed asparagus tips, tiny shrimp, minced fresh herbs, spring onions—all are perfectly suitable garnishes for *frittate*. The version below is a Roman classic: tiny artichoke hearts, dusted with Parmesan, baked into the eggs. Serve it as a first course or as a lunch or brunch dish. Then use the basic technique to launch you on your own inventions.

        8 large eggs
        1 tablespoon olive oil
        1 tablespoon butter
        4 small artichoke hearts in oil,
           halved (see left)
        2 tablespoons freshly grated
           Parmesan
           Salt and freshly ground
           black pepper
           Thinly sliced sweet red onion,
           for garnish
           Country-style Italian bread
           or Bruschetta (see page 13)

1. Preheat oven to 375° F. Beat eggs lightly. Heat oil and butter in a 9- or 10-inch nonstick skillet over moderately high heat. When fats are sizzling, add eggs and reduce heat to low. Arrange artichokes in a pretty pattern on top of eggs. Cook gently, lifting edges of frittata to let uncooked egg run underneath, until it is just set on top. Dust with Parmesan, salt, and pepper. Transfer skillet to oven and bake just until frittata is firm on top; do not overcook or it will be tough.

2. Cool in skillet, then slide onto serving platter and cut into wedges. The frittata can be eaten hot, warm, or at room temperature. Serve with raw onion and bread or Bruschetta.

Serves 4.

CROSTINI DI SALSICCE E POMODORI
Sausage and tomato toasts

Crostini are Italy's version of France's famous canapés: small bread rounds with all manner of savory toppings. They range from earthy to surpassingly elegant, with imagination and good taste the only limiting factors. A hearty sausage-and-ricotta mixture from Rome makes a fine crostini garnish; serve the toasts bubbling hot with cocktails or wine.

> ½ pound hot Italian sausage, loose or in links
> ½ cup finely minced onion
> 1 to 2 teaspoons finely minced garlic (amount depends on garlic in sausage)
> ½ cup ricotta
> 1 cup peeled, seeded, and coarsely chopped plum tomatoes (see page 29)
> 2 tablespoons minced fresh basil
> Salt and freshly ground black pepper
> 1 teaspoon fennel seed
> ¼ cup freshly grated Parmesan
> 16 slices baguette-type bread, cut on the diagonal ¼ inch thick
> 3 tablespoons minced parsley

1. Remove casing from link sausage. In a medium skillet over moderate heat, fry sausage until browned. Transfer sausage to a large bowl, leaving fat in skillet. Sauté onion and garlic until softened in sausage fat, (about 3 minutes). Add to sausage in bowl along with ricotta, tomatoes, basil, salt and pepper to taste, fennel seed, and 2 tablespoons of the Parmesan. Mix lightly but well.

2. Preheat broiler 5 minutes. Mound sausage mixture on bread slices; dust with remaining Parmesan and broil until bubbly. Garnish with minced parsley and serve hot.

Makes 16 rounds, enough to serve 8 with other antipasti.

Make-Ahead Tip Sausage mixture may be made a day ahead and stored in refrigerator. Bring to room temperature before using.

Special Note

ITALIAN WINES FOR EVERY OCCASION

The Italians are the largest per-capita wine consumers in the world, but they are also conscientious consumers. Alcoholism is rare in Italy because wine is always linked to the table. It is respected and regarded like staples such as olive oil, bread, and salt: A meal wouldn't be complete without it.

There are dozens of Italian wines that never make it to this country, but the major varieties are widely represented here. As you might expect in a country with such a broad range of soils and climates, Italian wines are remarkably diverse. For serving purposes, you'll want to know which types are light, fresh, and best served young (apéritif and seafood wines) and which are fuller, richer, and more likely to age well (chicken and red-meat wines).

Once you've learned the broad categories, experiment often to find the producers and varieties you prefer. A good wine merchant can direct you to the best vintages and the most highly regarded producers, but you should always let your palate be the final judge.

The following guidelines should help you choose an Italian wine to suit your meal.

□ Before dinner: Prosecco, a dry sparkling wine from the Veneto region, is widely available now and makes a refreshing *aperitivo*. A light, crisp white, such as a Soave or an Orvieto, also sharpens the appetite. The most popular Italian aperitivo, however, is vermouth, both sweet and dry. Vermouth is made from wine that has been flavored with roots, herbs, seeds, or other aromatics and given a bitter edge with quinine, then fortified with brandy, sweetened with sugar, and possibly colored with caramel. Vermouths vary a bit from one manufacturer to another; the recipes are closely guarded trade secrets. Martini & Rossi and Cinzano are two of the largest producers. Vermouth should be served chilled, straight up or over ice, with a dash of soda or lemon twist if desired.

□ With lean white fish and shellfish, simply baked, steamed or grilled; with goat cheeses; with vegetable antipasti: Choose a lean, crisp white wine such as a Cortese di Gavi, a Soave, a Lugana, an Orvieto, or a Verdicchio dei Castelli di Jesi.

□ With fish in sauce; with richer, oilier fish such as salmon; with seafood pasta or risotto; with Bel Paese cheese: Serve a full-bodied white such as Pinot Bianco, Pinot Grigio, Frascati, Arneis, Vernaccia di San Gimignano, or an Italian Chardonnay.

□ With picnic food, dry sausages, ham, cold roast chicken, pasta salads, provolone, and antipasti: Serve a light-bodied red or rosé, such as Bardolino, Valpolicella, Grignolino, Lambrusco, or a simple Chianti (not Classico or Riserva).

□ With chicken in sauce; veal; mushroom dishes; pasta with meat sauce; polenta or risotto with meat components; rabbit and pork; fontina and taleggio cheeses: Serve a medium-bodied red, such as Barbera d'Alba, Barbera d'Asti, Merlot, Nebbiolo d'Alba, Chianti and Chianti Classico, or Dolcetto d'Alba.

□ With game, lamb, or beef; with Parmesan, Gorgonzola, or aged Asiago cheeses: Choose a full-bodied red wine, such as Barolo, Barbaresco, Gattinara, Spanna, Chianti Classico Riserva, Brunello di Montalcino, Vino Nobile di Montepulciano, Tignanello, or Amarone.

Created at Harry's Bar in Venice, Carpaccio is an easy and elegant first course of thin-sliced beef. Here, it is garnished with herbed tomatoes and grated Parmesan.

CROSTINI DI POLENTA
Polenta crostini with anchovy butter

Crostini (little toasts) are usually based on bread, but northern Italians often replace the bread with polenta. First the polenta is chilled until firm, then it's cut into bite-sized shapes, spread with a seasoned butter, and reheated. The result is a memorable little nibble, open to dozens of variations: Mushroom butter, herb butter, or Gorgonzola butter could take the place of the anchovy butter, for instance. Serve with cocktails or a light red wine.

    2 tablespoons olive oil
    1 recipe Basic Polenta (see
       page 58)
    8 to 10 anchovy fillets packed
       in oil, drained
    8 tablespoons unsalted butter,
       at room temperature
    2 tablespoons minced parsley

1. Grease an 11- by 13-inch baking sheet with olive oil. Pour thickened Polenta onto oiled sheet and allow to cool completely.

2. When Polenta has cooled and hardened, cut out triangles, rounds, or squares with a cookie cutter or knife. In a food processor or blender, blend anchovies and butter.

3. Preheat oven to 400° F. Spread a little anchovy butter on each crostino, and arrange on a baking sheet and bake until butter is melted and Polenta is heated through. Dust with minced parsley; serve immediately.

Makes 25 to 32 crostini, depending on size and shape.

Make-Ahead Tip Polenta can be made, chilled, and cut up to 8 hours ahead. Cover with plastic wrap. Bring to room temperature before baking. Anchovy butter can be made several days ahead and stored, covered, in the refrigerator.

BAGNA CAUDA
Oil and garlic dip with bread and vegetables

This "hot bath" is a specialty of Italy's Piedmont region, where it is sometimes garnished with another specialty: shaved white truffles. Even without them, this dip is addictive and highly aromatic. The ingredients are few and simple, but they melt down into a rich bath for bread and vegetables.

    ½ cup olive oil
    1 tablespoon butter
    ½ tablespoon minced garlic
    2 ounces anchovy fillets, mashed
       Salt and freshly ground
       black pepper
    For dipping:
       Cubes of day-old Italian
       bread
       Whole artichokes, boiled and
       quartered, chokes removed
       Blanched cauliflower floret
       Raw fennel slices (see
       page 80)
       Raw carrot sticks
       Raw, sweet red-pepper strips
       Raw celery, pale inner
       stalks only
       Halved hard-cooked eggs
       Blanched asparagus spears

In a small skillet over moderate heat, heat oil and butter until bubbly. Add garlic. Cook over low heat until fragrant; do not allow garlic to brown. Add anchovies and cook, stirring, for 2 minutes. Remove from heat; add salt and pepper to taste. Transfer dip to a warm serving bowl or, preferably, keep warm in a chafing dish. Serve with a platter of bread and vegetables for dipping.

Makes about ½ cup.

CARPACCIO
Thinly pounded raw beef

To make *carpaccio*, lean raw beef is sliced and pounded tissue-thin, then dressed with Parmesan and a piquant vinaigrette. A popular Venetian restaurant dish, it is also easily made at home. You can slice the beef a couple of hours ahead and keep it between sheets of plastic wrap, but it's best to pound it just before serving. To make slicing easier, put meat in freezer until it is very cold but not frozen.

    1½ pounds beef tenderloin,
        trimmed of all fat
    1½ cups peeled, seeded,
        and chopped fresh tomato
        (see page 29)
    ½   cup minced Italian parsley
    ¼   cup minced fresh oregano
    ¼   cup minced fresh basil
    ⅓   cup fresh lemon juice
    3   to 4 tablespoons olive oil
    3   tablespoons freshly grated
        Parmesan
        Salt and freshly ground
        black pepper
    2   tablespoons minced fresh
        chives (optional)

1. Cut beef into 10 thin slices, approximately 2½ ounces each. Put each slice between two sheets of plastic wrap or waxed paper and pound with a mallet or the bottom of a skillet until beef is paper-thin.

2. In a bowl combine tomatoes, parsley, oregano, basil, and 1 tablespoon each of lemon juice and olive oil. Marinate at room temperature for at least 10 minutes or up to 1 hour.

3. To serve, arrange tenderloin slices on individual plates or large platters. Scatter tomatoes around them. Drizzle with remaining olive oil and lemon. Dust with Parmesan. Sprinkle salt and pepper over all and garnish with chives (if used).

Serves 10.

A TREASURY OF ITALIAN CHEESES

It would be impossible to count Italy's cheeses. With diligence, one might compile a list of the cheeses made at the country's many cooperatives. But how could one begin to count the cheeses made of small farms and sold only at local markets? It has been said, albeit jokingly, that there are as many sheep's-milk cheeses in Italy as there are shepherds!

Certainly Italian cheeses form a varied group, reflecting the soil, climate, and geography of the country's vastly different regions. The cheeses also embody methods and traditions handed down for centuries, some of them dating from Etruscan times.

Many of these marvelous cheeses never turn up in the United States because they're highly perishable. Ricotta, for example, must be eaten very fresh and thus is not a good candidate for export. But modern transport has meant that the range of cheeses available here is rapidly expanding. All of the following are obtainable in large cities, and most are carried by well-stocked cheese shops anywhere.

Asiago A cow's-milk cheese, young Asiago is nutty, rich, and slightly piquant. It makes a good table cheese; as it ages, it gets harder and sharper and can be grated. Many shops carry both young and aged Asiago.

Bel Paese A cow's-milk cheese that is creamy and mild, Bel Paese makes a good sandwich or snacking cheese. It melts well and can be used to top casseroles or in sauces. Be sure to buy the imported variety.

Caciocavallo This cow's-milk cheese is made in a pear shape and sometimes lightly smoked. When young, *caciocavallo* is mild but tangy; as it ages, it gets drier and sharper and is sometimes grated.

Caprino *Caprino* is a generic term for goat's-milk cheese. Caprini are usually soft, mild, and spreadable when young, tangier and drier as they age. They are delicious sprinkled with black pepper and olive oil.

Fontina Made from cow's milk, fontina is one of Italy's foremost cheeses. It is creamy and smooth, with tiny holes, a nutty flavor, and an earthy aroma. Fontina is an excellent cooking cheese.

Gorgonzola A cow's-milk cheese, Gorgonzola is undoubtedly Italy's most famous blue-veined cheese. Its texture is creamy and moist, its flavor pungent. It is delicious with pears and peaches, in creamy pasta sauces, and mixed half-and-half with butter as a spread for crackers.

Mascarpone A cow's-milk cheese that must be eaten very fresh, *mascarpone* is luxuriously smooth and creamy, a bit like whipped butter or stiffly whipped cream. It is often sweetened slightly and served for dessert with strawberries, pears, or peaches. Some cheese shops carry a savory *torta* (cake) *di mascarpone* made of layers of the creamy cheese interspersed with layers of provolone, basil, and pine nuts.

Mozzarella Originally made from water-buffalo milk, mozzarella is now primarily a cow's-milk cheese. However, a few shops in major cities import an authentic *mozzarella di bufala*. Both varieties must be eaten very fresh and should be purchased from merchants with a rapid turnover. Mozzarella is perfect for pizza, of course, as well as for sandwiches and salads. Sliced and served with ripe tomatoes, fresh basil, olive oil, salt, and pepper, mozzarella makes a classic summer salad. The packaged domestic varieties bear little resemblance to the real thing.

Parmigiano Reggiano This cow's-milk cheese is one of Italy's most famous exports. Real *Parmigiano* is made within a strictly delimited region and according to strictly controlled methods. It is nutty, golden, and sharp, with a moist texture that gets drier as it ages. Young Parmigiano is a lovely after-dinner cheese with pears or toasted nuts; the aged version is the classic grating cheese for pasta, pizza, soups, and casseroles. Always buy your Parmesan in chunks and grate it just before using. Leftover rinds can be simmered in soups for added flavor. Domestic Parmesan is a poor substitute and not suitable for recipes in this book.

Pecorino Romano The best-known of the *pecorino* (sheep's-milk) cheeses, *Pecorino Romano* is pale, moist, and sliceable when young, becoming sharper and harder as it ages. Older pecorino makes a tangy grating cheese. When young, it is delicious with olive oil, olives, prosciutto, and bread.

Provolone A cow's-milk cheese, provolone is mild, firm, and sliceable. It is good for snacking and melts well on pizza. Smoked provolone makes an especially good ham-and-cheese sandwich.

Ricotta A cow's-milk cheese made from whey, ricotta is mild, creamy, and moist and should be used when very fresh. It is an important ingredient in many dishes, from lasagne and cannelloni to cheesecake, but it is also delightful on its own. Sprinkled with sugar and cinnamon or cocoa and served with seasonal fruits, it makes a lovely dessert.

Ricotta Salata This sheep's-milk cheese has a distinctive, sharp tang. It makes a delicious lunch, sliced and served with sausage, olives, bread, and olive oil.

Robiola This is the name of a family of cheeses made from cow's, goat's or sheep's milk, or a combination. They are generally soft, fresh, and creamy. However, some versions are mild; others are quite pungent. Ask to taste before you buy.

Taleggio A cow's-milk cheese, *taleggio* is one of Italy's best. When well made and ripe, it is soft and creamy with a distinct aroma of truffles. It makes a splendid after-dinner cheese with fruit and bread.

FONTINA FRITTA
Fontina fritters

Golden brown outside and molten within, these Roman fritters are a heavenly mouthful. The batter may be made ahead, but the cheese must be fried at the last minute. Serve with a crisp white wine, such as an Orvieto or a Soave.

> ¾ pound chilled fontina, not too ripe
> ¼ cup dry white wine
> 2 egg yolks
> 1 teaspoon minced garlic
> 1 teaspoon baking powder
> 1½ cups flour
>   Salt
> 2½ tablespoons olive oil
> ½ to ⅔ cup ice water
>   Vegetable oil, for deep-frying
> 2 egg whites
> ½ cup minced fresh basil

1. Cut cheese into 1-inch cubes. In a bowl whisk together wine, egg yolks, and garlic. Whisk in baking powder, flour, and 1 teaspoon salt. Whisk in olive oil, then add enough ice water to make a thick but pourable batter, about the consistency of pancake batter. Let rest at room temperature for 2 hours.

2. When ready to serve, heat 2 inches of vegetable oil in a frying pan to 360° F. Beat egg whites with a pinch of salt until stiff but not dry. Fold into batter along with basil.

3. Dip cheese cubes into batter. Allow excess batter to drip off; fry chunks in oil until uniformly golden. Drain fritters on paper towels; salt lightly. Serve immediately.

Serves 8 with 2 or 3 other antipasti.

Make-Ahead Tip Batter, minus beaten egg whites, may be mixed a day ahead. Cover and refrigerate; bring to room temperature before adding egg whites and using.

RICOTTA SALATA E PROSCIUTTO
Ricotta salata and prosciutto

Ricotta salata (also known as *ricotta pecorino*) isn't easy to find, but it's worth looking for. Sicilians serve it as an antipasto, with warm bread and a drizzle of olive oil. If necessary, substitute imported feta cheese.

> 1 pound ricotta salata
> ½ pound prosciutto, sliced as thin as possible
> 3 tablespoons (approximately) olive oil
>   Freshly ground black pepper
> 2 tablespoons minced parsley
> 2 tablespoons freshly grated Parmesan (optional)
> 8 large or 16 small pieces hot, country-style bread

Slice ricotta salata thinly. (If you use feta, break it into chunks.) Arrange cheese on a rustic serving platter or on individual plates. Surround with slices of prosciutto. Drizzle olive oil and grind pepper over all. Sprinkle with parsley and Parmesan (if used). If feta is very salty, omit Parmesan. Serve with hot bread.

Serves 8.

Dip cubes of fontina cheese in batter, then fry until crisp and brown. The piping-hot Fontina Fritta makes a fine appetizer, served with chilled white wine and herbed olives.

Legumi in Pinzimonio pairs the season's freshest produce with a fine olive oil for a light and brightly colored first course. For a more elaborate antipasto, add a selection of cured meats (see Italy's Cured Meats and Sausages, opposite page) and a loaf of bread.

CIPOLLE AL FORNO
Roasted balsamic onions

Small boiling onions (not pearl onions) are the perfect size for an antipasto. In Modena, they are baked until tender, then glazed with their sweet-and-sour baking juices to make an unusual accompaniment to smoked sliced meats (see opposite page) or fontina. They should be served with a knife and fork and eaten directly from their hard outer skin. Accompany roasted balsamic onions with chunks of warm Italian country bread.

> 2 dozen small boiling onions, about 2 inches in diameter
> ½ to ⅔ cup olive oil
> ⅓ cup balsamic vinegar
> Salt and freshly ground black pepper
> 2 tablespoons minced Italian parsley, for garnish

1. Preheat oven to 350° F. Remove outermost skin of onions, leaving a hard, inedible exterior. Put onions in a bowl. Add enough olive oil to nearly cover them; toss to coat.

2. Transfer onions to a roasting pan, reserving oil. Bake, basting onions occasionally with reserved oil, until onions are tender when pierced with a knife. Baking time depends on onion size, but onions will probably be done in 45 minutes to 1 hour and 15 minutes. Transfer onions to a plate and let cool.

3. Place roasting pan over a medium-hot burner and add vinegar. Reduce liquid to a dark, hazy syrup. Pour syrup over onions. Season to taste with salt and pepper and sprinkle with parsley. Serve cool.

Serves 8.

CAPONATINA
Eggplant relish

Sicily's sweet-and-sour dishes are enjoyed throughout Italy, with *caponatina* a particular favorite. It's an eggplant relish of wonderfully complex flavors and textures, to be scooped up with hearts of lettuce or chunks of bread. Hot and cool, sweet and tart, smooth and crunchy—it's all there in this beguiling dish.

> 3 large eggplants or 6 small Japanese eggplants
> 1½ cups olive oil
> 3 cups minced onions
> ⅓ cup minced garlic
> 1 cup diced celery
> 2 cups peeled and seeded tomatoes in ½-inch chunks (see page 29)
> 3 tablespoons capers
> ⅔ cup minced carrot
> ½ cup toasted pine nuts
> 2 cups oil-cured black olives
> ⅓ cup sugar
> ⅔ cup red wine vinegar
> ½ teaspoon cayenne pepper, or more to taste
> Salt
> ⅔ cup minced parsley
> Additional olive oil, for garnish
> Additional minced parsley, for garnish

1. Preheat oven to 375° F. Peel eggplants and cut into ½-inch dice. Oil a large baking sheet or roasting pan with 3 tablespoons of the olive oil. Toss eggplant with ¾ cup of the olive oil to coat well, then transfer eggplant to baking sheet or pan. Bake, tossing eggplant frequently, until it is soft and lightly browned (about 20 minutes).

2. While eggplant is baking, heat remaining oil in a large skillet over moderate heat. Add onions and garlic and sauté until soft (7 to 10 minutes); do not allow garlic to brown. Add celery, tomatoes, capers, carrot, pine nuts, olives, sugar, vinegar, and cayenne. Simmer slowly 30 minutes. Add salt to taste. Add eggplant and cook an additional 10 minutes. Add the

⅔ cup parsley and let cool. Taste again and correct seasoning. To serve, transfer to a bowl, drizzle with olive oil and garnish with minced parsley.

Serves 12.

LEGUMI IN PINZIMONIO
Raw vegetables with olive-oil dip

Tuscans show off their finest oil and their freshest vegetables by serving them *in pinzimonio*. You're offered a basket or a platter of crisp and colorful raw vegetables, along with a bowl of the best oil seasoned with nothing but salt and pepper. You "pinch" (*pinzare*) the vegetables and join them in "marriage" (*matrimonio*) with the oil. If the oil is top-notch, there is no finer dip.

> 2 cups fruity olive oil
> Coarse salt
> Freshly ground black pepper
> Lemon wedges, for garnish
> For dipping:
> Sliced bulb fennel (see page 80)
> Cherry tomatoes
> Carrot sticks
> Innermost celery stalks
> Endive leaves
> Cucumber spears, seeded
> Innermost hearts of baby artichokes (see page 16)
> Hearts of small lettuces
> Spears of young tender zucchini

Season olive oil to taste with salt and pepper. Divide oil among small dipping bowls, one to a person. Arrange vegetables for dipping on a large, rustic platter. Offer each guest a dipping bowl, lemon wedges, and a small salad plate. Or you can pour a little seasoned oil on each salad plate, arrange a bouquet of raw vegetables on top, and garnish the plate with a lemon wedge.

Serves 8.

ITALY'S CURED MEATS AND SAUSAGES

In Italy cooks avail themselves of a large collection of cured meats for antipasto, sandwiches, and other dishes. Unfortunately, at this writing, American law prohibits importation of these meats. However, domestic versions can be found in delis, specialty shops, and Italian markets. The following are the most widely available. Thinly sliced coppa, mortadella, prosciutto, and salami are all appropriate for an antipasto platter.

Coppa is the cured foreshank of a pig. It has a sweet-salty flavor.

Italian-style link sausage is made from fresh-ground pork highly seasoned with salt, garlic, and wine. "Hot" varieties have a generous lacing of hot red pepper; "sweet" varieties usually include fennel seed instead. They may be grilled and served with peppers or crumbled and used for pizza, pasta sauces, or stuffings.

Mortadella is the original "bologna." It is a large, round, fine-grained sausage studded with fat.

Pancetta is unsmoked bacon made from pork belly. It is seasoned with salt, pepper, and spices, then rolled into a sausage shape and cured. Buy it in slices, uncoil them to make long baconlike strips, then slice as the recipe directs. American bacon, because it is smoked, is not a close substitute.

Prosciutto is a salted and air-cured hind ham. It has a sweet, nutty taste and a velvety texture. Often served as an antipasto with melon, figs, or pears, it may also be used in sandwiches and pasta sauces, on pizzas, in stuffings, and in sautéed dishes.

Salami are air-dried sausages made from seasoned pork or beef. One of the best known is Genoa salami, made with garlic and white peppercorns.

Basil and beans, cheese and onions—from such basic elements the Italians make their flavorful soups.

Soups

Italian soups range from delicate broths, such as Zuppa Pavese (see page 26), to hearty meal-in-a-bowl preparations such as Pasta e Fagioli (see page 28). This chapter offers recipes for some of Italy's most tantalizing soups. They span the seasons, from an autumn Sicilian pumpkin soup (see page 27) to a spring minestrone (see page 28). You'll also find (on page 29) an illustrated step-by-step explanation of how to peel, seed, and chop tomatoes—a technique essential to Italian cooking.

Egg and spinach pastas are the whimsical "straw and hay" of Bologna's famous Paglia e Fieno, traditionally dressed with cream and peas. The colorful noodles can also combine in a meaty broth, as shown here, accompanied by bread and sliced Parmesan in olive oil.

SOUPS

Soups play an important role in the Italians' daily diet, frequently taking the place of pasta as the first course of the main meal and often served as the main course at a light supper. They range from the delicate Zuppa Pavese (below) to the rib-sticking Pasta e Fagioli (see page 28), which is almost more a stew than a soup. In between are the various fish and shellfish soups, such as Zuppa di Vongole con Pomodori (see page 29), and the hearty seasonal minestrones (Minestrone Primavera appears on page 28). The rustic bread-based soups, such as Pappa al Pomodoro (see page 30), are among the most humble and delicious in the Italian repertoire.

ZUPPA PAVESE
Egg soup, Pavia style

This elegant soup can be made in minutes if you have the raw materials at hand: good bread, imported Parmesan, fresh eggs, and rich stock. You simply pour the simmering stock over toast, cheese, and eggs and allow the eggs to cook in the soup. If you prefer your eggs more fully cooked, poach them first before placing them in the soup bowls.

- 10 cups rich unsalted chicken stock
- 16 bread rounds, about 2 inches in diameter and ¼ inch thick, made from dense homemade, country-style bread
- 6 tablespoons (approximately) clarified butter
- 16 eggs
  Salt, to taste
  Freshly grated Parmesan, for garnish

Bring stock to a boil. While stock is heating fry bread rounds in batches in clarified butter until golden and crisp on both sides (about 10 minutes). Put 2 bread rounds in each of 8 warm bowls. Break 2 eggs into each bowl, being careful not to break the yolks. Season with salt; dust lightly with Parmesan. Carefully pour the bubbling stock over eggs. Serve immediately, with extra Parmesan on the side.

Makes about 10 cups, 8 servings.

ZUPPA DI RISO E BIETOLE
Rice and chard soup

This light Bolognese vegetable soup could precede an Arrosto di Maiale con Rosmarino (see page 84), a split grilled chicken, or pan-fried sausages.

> 2 large bunches fresh green or red chard
> ¼ cup olive oil
> ¼ cup minced onion
> 3 cups (approximately) rich chicken stock
> ½ cup Italian Arborio rice
> ⅓ cup fresh basil leaves
> Freshly grated Parmesan

1. Wash chard well. Remove stems and cut them into ¼-inch pieces. Bring a large pot of salted water to a boil and blanch the chard leaves for 10 to 15 seconds. Transfer them with a large slotted spoon to ice water, then drain, squeeze dry, and chop coarsely. Blanch the stems in the same boiling water, refresh them in ice water, then drain and dry.

2. Heat oil in a stockpot over moderate heat. Add onion and sauté until translucent and soft (about 3 to 5 minutes). Add chard stems and stir to coat with oil. Add chicken stock and rice and bring to a simmer. Cover and simmer gently 15 minutes or until rice is just cooked. Add chopped chard and heat through gently. If rice has absorbed most of stock, add a little more, but soup should be thick.

3. To serve, cut the basil into a fine julienne. Divide soup among warm bowls and garnish with julienned basil and Parmesan.

Makes 7 or 8 cups, 6 to 8 servings.

SOPA DI ZUCCA
Sicilian pumpkin soup

For best results, make this soup with small, sweet sugar pumpkins. The big, watery Halloween pumpkins will give inferior results.

> 3 tablespoons olive oil
> 3 small carrots, peeled and diced
> 2½ cups diced red onion
> 1 medium leek, washed and sliced
> 1 parsnip, peeled and diced
> 1 pound small, sweet pumpkin, peeled and cut into approximately 2-inch cubes
> 4 cups rich, homemade chicken stock
> 2 teaspoons grated lemon rind
> 3 tablespoons lemon juice
> 1 teaspoon dried oregano
> ¼ teaspoon hot red-pepper flakes
> 1 cup milk
> Salt and freshly ground black pepper
> 3 tablespoons minced parsley mixed with 1 tablespoon grated lemon rind, for garnish

1. Heat olive oil in a large stockpot over moderate heat. Add carrots, onion, leek, and parsnip; sauté 5 minutes. Add pumpkin, chicken stock, lemon rind, lemon juice, oregano, and pepper flakes. Cover and simmer until pumpkin is tender. Cool slightly.

2. Transfer mixture in batches to a blender and blend, adding milk as necessary to facilitate blending (you should use the entire cup). Return soup to stockpot. Season to taste with salt and pepper. Soup should be peppery. Reheat and serve garnished with parsley-lemon rind mixture.

Makes about 12 cups, 10 generous servings.

PAGLIA E FIENO IN BRODO
"Straw and hay" in broth, Bolognese style

When egg pasta and spinach pasta are tossed in a cream sauce with peas and prosciutto, the result is the *paglia e fieno* ("straw and hay") of Piacenza. The same combination of yellow and green produces a striking first-course soup, the colorful noodles afloat in a rich meat broth. It makes an elegant introduction to almost any main course. For a more casual meal, begin with an *antipasto* assortment and serve the soup as the main event with bread and sliced Parmesan marinated in olive oil.

> 1 quart homemade beef or chicken stock
> 3½ ounces fresh spinach fettuccine (use Pasta Verde, page 34), in 6-inch lengths
> 3½ ounces fresh egg fettuccine (use Pasta Gialla, page 34), in 6-inch lengths
> Salt
> 2 ounces freshly grated Parmesan

1. Bring stock to a simmer in a large stockpot. In a separate pot, bring a large amount of salted water to a boil. Add both spinach and egg fettuccine and cook until just wilted, about 20 to 25 seconds. Drain and run under cold water to remove any starch. Transfer pasta to the simmering stock and simmer until pasta is al dente. Season broth to taste with salt.

2. Ladle soup into warm serving bowls and top each serving with grated Parmesan.

Makes about 7 cups, 4 to 6 servings.

PASTA E FAGIOLI
Pasta and bean soup

Perhaps the only soup that's better than a good *pasta e fagioli* is a pasta e fagioli the second day. This thick, rustic soup is practically a staple in Tuscan homes and a good example of how Italian cooks turn nothing much into something wonderful. If you make it a day ahead, wait to add the pasta until just before you serve it. And if you use homemade pasta, be sure to shake off any excess flour before adding it to the soup.

> 2 cups dried Great Northern white beans or cannellini beans
> ¼ cup olive oil
> 2 ounces pancetta, diced
> 1 cup coarsely chopped onion
> ½ cup diced celery
> ½ cup diced carrot
> 1½ tablespoons sliced garlic
> 9 cups water
> 4½ cups peeled, seeded, and diced tomatoes (see opposite page)
> Salt and freshly ground black pepper
> 5 ounces pasta, either day-old homemade wide-ribbon noodles or fettuccine (use any of the doughs on pages 34–35) or dried shells or bow ties
> Freshly grated Parmesan
> ¼ cup (approximately) extravirgin olive oil

1. Soak beans overnight in water to cover (no need to refrigerate). The next day heat the ¼ cup olive oil in a large stockpot over moderate heat. Add pancetta and render slightly (about 3 minutes). Add onion and sauté until soft and translucent (about 3 minutes). Add celery, carrot, and garlic and sauté gently another 5 minutes, stirring occasionally.

2. Drain beans and add to pot along with the 9 cups fresh water and tomatoes. Cover and simmer 1½ hours, or until beans are tender. Season to taste with salt and pepper. If you are using homemade pasta, add it to the soup and cook until tender. If you are using dried pasta, cook it until tender in boiling salted water;

drain it well, add to soup, and heat through. Cool soup slightly before serving. Serve it in warm bowls, topped with a sprinkle of Parmesan and a drizzle of extravirgin olive oil.

Makes 12 to 14 cups, about 12 servings.

MINESTRONE PRIMAVERA
Spring minestrone

A chunky soup chock-full of vegetables often opens an Italian meal, both in homes and in restaurants. It can be made ahead—in fact, it's best made ahead—and it can be served hot, warm, or at room temperature. Put a cruet of extravirgin olive oil on the table for guests to add at will, and follow the soup with a simple roast of lamb or chicken. A hearty minestrone makes a great Sunday supper, with crusty bread, a light red wine, and a fruit dessert. The version that follows is from Bologna.

> 3 tablespoons olive oil
> 1 cup cubed pancetta (½-inch pieces)
> 1 cup minced onion
> 2 small leeks, white part only, well washed and thinly sliced
> 3 cups coarsely shredded inner cabbage leaves
> 4 cups peeled, seeded, and chopped tomatoes (see opposite page)
> 12 small new potatoes, quartered
> 5 cups chicken broth
> 2 cups carrots in ½-inch-thick rounds
> ¾ cup chopped bulb fennel (see page 80)
> 1 cup cooked and drained kidney beans
> 1 cup cooked and drained garbanzo beans (chick-peas)
> 1 cup fresh green beans, preferably Italian beans, in 1-inch pieces
> 2 cups tiny cauliflower florets
> 2 cups cooked and drained small shell pasta or macaroni
> 2 cups fresh shelled peas
> Salt and freshly ground black pepper
> ½ cup minced Italian parsley
> Freshly grated Parmesan

1. Heat 2 tablespoons of the olive oil in a large stock pot. Add pancetta and fry gently for 4 minutes. Add onion and leeks and cook 5 minutes, or until onion is soft and translucent but not browned.

2. Add 1 tablespoon oil to the pot and add the cabbage. Stir to coat cabbage with oil, then sauté 1 minute. Add tomatoes, potatoes, and 3 cups of the broth. Bring to a simmer and cook 10 minutes. Add carrots, fennel, and ½ cup more stock. Simmer 10 minutes.

3. Add remaining stock, kidney and garbanzo beans, fresh beans, cauliflower, and pasta. Simmer 10 minutes. Add peas. Continue simmering until potatoes are fully cooked and peas are crisp-tender. Pasta should be cooked slightly beyond al dente.

4. Season to taste with salt and pepper. Stir in half the parsley. Serve soup in warm bowls, garnishing with remaining parsley and Parmesan. Pass additional Parmesan at the table.

Makes about 12 cups, about 8 servings.

ZUPPA DI VONGOLE CON POMODORI
Neapolitan clam soup with tomatoes

To reproduce this soup as it's made on the Naples waterfront, you'll need the tiny Italian clams called *vongole*. Lacking those, choose any small fresh clams and do your best to find fresh Italian parsley. Serve this fragrant soup/stew with plenty of bread to soak up the juices, a bowl for the shells, and a bottle of Verdicchio or Sicilian Corvo.

> 3 to 4 pounds small, fresh clams
> 2 tablespoons cornmeal
> ½ cup olive oil
> ½ cup chopped onion
> ¼ teaspoon hot red-pepper flakes
> 2 tablespoons minced garlic
> 4 large tomatoes, peeled, seeded, and diced (See Step-by-Step at right)
> 2 tablespoons chopped fresh oregano
> 3 tablespoons minced Italian parsley
> Fresh coarsely cracked black pepper

1. Scrub clams well and put in a large pot of salted water along with cornmeal. Refrigerate 3 to 4 hours to purge clams. Drain clams and discard any that have already opened.

2. Heat olive oil in a large stockpot over moderate heat and add onion, pepper flakes, and garlic. Sauté gently until onions are slightly softened, about 3 minutes. Add tomatoes and sauté 7 or 8 minutes, then add oregano and half of the parsley. Add clams, cover, and steam, shaking pan occasionally, until clams are opened, about 5 to 7 minutes.

3. Divide clams and tomato broth among four warm bowls. Garnish with remaining parsley and pass the cracked black pepper.

Serves 4.

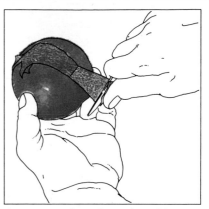

PEELING, SEEDING, AND CHOPPING TOMATOES

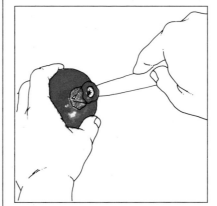

1. *Use a paring knife to core the tomatoes.*

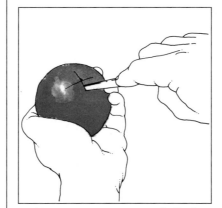

2. *Turn tomatoes over and slit the skin in an X-shaped cut.*

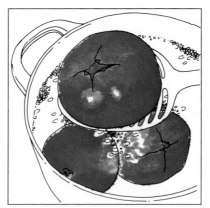

3. *Put the tomatoes in a pan containing enough boiling water to cover them and boil for 15 seconds. Remove them with a slotted spoon and put them in a bowl of cold water. Leave for a few seconds.*

4. *Remove them from the cold water and use a paring knife to pull off the skins.*

5. *Halve the tomatoes horizontally with a chopping knife. Hold each half over a bowl, cut side down, and squeeze to remove the seeds.*

6. *Chop the tomatoes into small pieces.*

MINESTRA DI FUNGHI
Mushroom soup

The dried Italian mushrooms called *porcini* (see page 9) add an earthy flavor to this rustic Piedmontese soup. Save any leftover soaking liquid to flavor other soups, sauces, or stews.

- 1 ounce dried Italian porcini mushrooms
- 1½ cups hot water
- 1½ tablespoons unsalted butter
- 1½ tablespoons minced garlic, plus 1 cut clove
- ¾ cup thinly sliced onion
- 2 teaspoons flour
- 6 tablespoons dry white wine
- 4 cups chicken stock
- 4 ounces fresh mushrooms, cleaned and quartered
  Salt and freshly ground black pepper
- 6 bread rounds, about 2 inches in diameter and ⅓ inch thick, cut from dense, day-old country-style bread
  Olive oil
- ½ cup chopped fresh lemon pulp
- ½ cup minced parsley

1. Soak porcini in the hot water 20 minutes. Carefully lift mushrooms out with a slotted spoon. Strain liquid through cheesecloth and reserve. Pick through porcini carefully to remove any grit. Chop coarsely.

2. Heat butter in a large stockpot over moderate heat. Add the minced garlic and onion; sauté until onion is soft and translucent, about 5 minutes. Add flour and wine; cook gently 5 minutes. Add stock, porcini, and 2 tablespoons of the reserved porcini liquid. Cook 5 minutes. Add fresh mushrooms and cook until they are very tender. Season to taste with salt and pepper.

3. Preheat oven to 350° F. Rub bread rounds with the cut clove of garlic, brush well with olive oil, and toast in oven until browned and fragrant. Add lemon pulp and half of the parsley to the soup; reheat gently. Put a bread round in the bottom of each of 6 warm bowls, ladle soup over, and garnish with remaining parsley.

Makes about 5 cups, about 6 servings.

PAPPA AL POMODORO
Tuscan-style bread soup with greens and tomatoes

Because this soup has so few ingredients, it requires the best: vine-ripened summer tomatoes and dense, chewy, homemade or homestyle bread. It's a popular summer soup in the *trattorie* of Florence, where it often precedes a hefty Bistecca alla Fiorentina (see page 76). It can be served either hot or at room temperature.

- ½ cup plus 2 tablespoons olive oil
- 2 tablespoons thinly sliced garlic
- 4 cups peeled, seeded, and diced tomatoes (see page 29)
- 2 cups arugula, washed, or 1½ cups blanched turnip greens
- 2 cups day-old bread, in 2-inch cubes
- 3 cups water
  Salt and freshly ground black pepper

For garnish:
- 8 one-inch bread cubes (optional; see step 2)
  Olive oil
  Arugula leaves, torn into small pieces

1. Heat ½ cup of the olive oil in a 4-quart pot over moderately low heat. Add garlic and sauté until fragrant. Add tomatoes and cook gently until they begin to exude their liquid (about 7 or 8 minutes). Add arugula and let wilt 3 to 4 minutes. Add remaining 2 tablespoons oil, the 2-inch bread cubes, and the water. Cover the pot and set aside 10 minutes. The bread will absorb most of the water.

2. Season to taste with salt and pepper. *To serve at room temperature:* Garnish with a swirl of olive oil and a few arugula leaves. *To serve hot:* Fry 1-inch bread cubes in olive oil until they are golden and crisp. Divide hot bread cubes among soup bowls and pour soup over them. Garnish with olive oil and arugula.

Makes about 10 cups, 10 to 12 first-course servings, 4 to 6 main-course servings.

ZUPPA DI POMODORO
Sicilian summer tomato soup

Among Italians, only a Sicilian would think to add spices, sugar, and orange to a tomato soup! Make it with sweet, vine-ripened tomatoes and follow it with a grilled or baked fish.

- ¼ cup unsalted butter
- 2 tablespoons olive oil
- 2 red onions, chopped
- 2 yellow onions, chopped
- 1 bunch green onions, minced
- ½ cup minced carrot
- ½ cup minced celery
- ¼ cup minced garlic
- 1 cup coarsely chopped parsley
  Pinch cinnamon
  Pinch nutmeg
- 2 tablespoons tomato paste
- 1½ pounds fresh spinach
- 18 plum tomatoes, peeled and chopped (see page 29)
- 1 teaspoon sugar
  Grated rind of 1 orange
- ¼ cup fresh orange juice
- 4 cups chicken stock
- 1 cup dry white wine
- ½ cup small fresh basil leaves
  Salt, freshly ground black pepper, and cayenne pepper

1. Heat butter and olive oil in a large pot over moderate heat. Add red and yellow onions; sauté about 5 minutes, until soft and translucent. Add green onions, carrot, celery, garlic, parsley, cinnamon, nutmeg, and tomato paste. Stir and cook 5 minutes.

2. Wash spinach and remove stems. Blanch leaves briefly in boiling water. Shock leaves in ice water to stop the cooking. Drain well; chop coarsely.

3. Add chopped tomatoes, spinach, sugar, orange rind, and orange juice to pot. Add stock and wine. Bring to a simmer and cook 10 to 15 minutes. Stir in basil and remove from heat. Purée soup in a blender in batches. Return to pot; season to taste with salt, pepper, and cayenne. Reheat and divide among warm bowls to serve.

Makes about 9 cups, 8 to 10 first-course servings, 4 main-course servings.

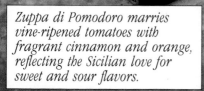

Zuppa di Pomodoro marries vine-ripened tomatoes with fragrant cinnamon and orange, reflecting the Sicilian love for sweet and sour flavors.

Pasta may be either dried or fresh; it also may be flavored with herbs or vegetables. Whatever its form, there's a wealth of sauces to top it.

Pasta & Sauces

To many Americans, the heart of Italian cooking is pasta in all its forms. Spaghetti, lasagne, cannelloni, ravioli, fettuccine—these are the dishes we love. This chapter presents the basics—pasta doughs and sauces—and the dishes made from them. The familiar favorites are all here, with some interesting new twists, such as dried-mushroom sauce in lasagne (see page 42) and potatoes mixed with pesto and *pappardelle* (see page 41). There are helpful step-by-step photographs showing how to form tortellini (page 38) and ravioli (page 43). A menu for a hearty Sicilian country dinner completes the chapter.

PASTA, FRESH AND DRIED

Pasta has graced the Italian table since before Marco Polo, and it is now eaten from one end of "the boot" to the other. Northern Italian pasta dishes are usually based on a fresh Pasta Gialla (at right); southern Italians eat considerably more dried pasta, made with only durum (hard wheat) flour and water. The south is historically a poor region, and possibly families couldn't afford the luxury of eggs in their pasta dough. In any case, the best dried pasta today is made in the factories of southern Italy and exported all over the world.

The variety of pasta shapes (see page 7) is surpassed only by the variety of sauces. And the Italian cook is very careful to match the right shape to the right sauce! Hearty meat sauces are best with a sturdy dried pasta, especially a shape—like a shell or a ridged tube—that can trap bits of the sauce. Soft fresh noodles are the choice for delicate cream sauces and butter-based sauces and for floating in soups.

A food processor makes the job of mixing fresh dough much faster, although the dough can easily be mixed and kneaded by hand. Rolling out the dough, however, is a tedious task by hand. If you plan to make pasta regularly, a hand-cranked pasta machine is a practical investment.

DOUGHS FOR HOMEMADE PASTA

Fresh homemade pasta doughs are made with eggs for easy handling. The egg provides the only moisture and makes the dough softer and easier to knead than a flour-and-water dough. Pasta Gialla (Basic Egg Dough) is probably the one you will use most often. However, the dough can also be varied with the addition of cooked spinach, fresh herbs, grated lemon rind, or puréed sun-dried tomatoes. The flavored doughs are a fun twist, but take care to serve them with complementary sauces. Suggestions precede each recipe.

Each of the following recipes yields about 1¼ pounds of pasta. If the dish you are making calls for less, don't throw away the leftover dough. Consider these possibilities:

☐ Wrap it and freeze for later use; it will keep indefinitely.

☐ Roll it out and cut into shapes for soup that day or the next.

☐ Roll it out, cut into uniform shapes, allow to dry on racks, and then store in an airtight container. Use it as you would any dried pasta.

☐ Roll, cut, and cook the leftovers immediately; use them in a cold pasta salad.

PASTA GIALLA
Basic egg dough

- 1½ cups unbleached flour
- 1 teaspoon coarse salt
- 1½ large eggs (see Note) or 2 medium eggs, lightly beaten

To mix by hand: Put flour and salt in a bowl. Stir to blend. Make a well in the center and add the eggs. With a fork or with your fingertips, gradually incorporate all the flour to form a mass. Knead lightly to form a smooth ball. Cover with plastic wrap and let rest 20 minutes or overnight before rolling and cutting. *To mix in a food processor:* Put flour and salt in work bowl of processor fitted with steel blade. Begin processing. With the machine running, add eggs through the feed tube in a slow, steady stream. Process until mixture begins to come together but has not formed a ball. Stop machine and press a bit of

dough between thumb and first finger. If it holds together, remove dough from bowl and knead by hand to form a smooth ball. If it doesn't hold together, process another 5 seconds, then knead by hand to form a smooth ball. Cover with plastic wrap and let rest 20 minutes or overnight before rolling and cutting.

Makes 1¼ pounds pasta.

Note Break 2 large eggs into a bowl. Whisk with a fork to blend. Measure volume and pour off one quarter.

PASTA VERDE
Spinach pasta

Be sure to squeeze as much moisture as possible out of the spinach or the dough will be too wet. Serve spinach fettuccine with Ragù Bolognese (see page 36) or use it to make a colorful lasagne.

- 1 recipe Pasta Gialla (at left)
- ¾ pound fresh spinach, leaves and stems, blanched, drained, squeezed dry, and finely minced

To mix by hand: Combine flour and salt as directed for Pasta Gialla. Combine spinach and eggs. Make a well in the flour and add spinach-egg mixture. Continue as directed for Pasta Gialla. *To mix in a food processor:* Place spinach in work bowl of food processor along with flour and salt. Process until blended, then add eggs and continue as directed for Pasta Gialla.

Makes 1¼ pounds pasta.

PASTA DI HERBE
Fresh herb pasta

Fresh herbs from your garden or market can turn Pasta Gialla into a fragrant pasta that's delicious with just butter and cheese. Or use buttered herb pasta as a bed for a saucy stew, such as Osso Buco (see page 77). Be careful with strong herbs like rosemary and oregano; use them in small quantities, rounding out the cup of herbs called for with mild parsley.

- 1 recipe Pasta Gialla (opposite page)
- 1 cup mixed fresh herbs (basil, chives, parsley, chervil), loosely packed

To mix by hand: Combine flour and salt as directed for Pasta Gialla. Mince herbs and combine with beaten egg. Make a well in the center of the flour and add the herb-egg mixture. Continue as directed for Pasta Gialla. *To mix in a food processor:* Mince herbs and place in work bowl of food processor fitted with the steel blade. Add flour and salt. Process until blended, then add eggs and continue as directed for Pasta Gialla.

Makes 1¼ pounds pasta.

PASTA DI LIMONE
Lemon pasta

Serve this zesty pasta with steamed mussels or seafood sauces. Dressed with olive oil and parsley, it could partner a simple roast chicken or a veal stew. Use only the bright yellow part of the lemon rind; the white part is bitter.

- 1 recipe Pasta Gialla (opposite page)
- 1½ tablespoons grated lemon rind
- ½ teaspoon lemon juice

To mix by hand: Combine flour and salt as directed for Pasta Gialla. Combine lemon rind and juice with eggs, then make a well in the center of the flour and add the egg-lemon mixture. Continue as directed for Pasta Gialla. *To mix in a food processor:* Place lemon rind in work bowl of food processor along with flour and salt. Process until blended. Combine lemon juice with eggs, then add to flour and continue as directed for Pasta Gialla.

Makes 1¼ pounds pasta.

PASTA DI POMODORI
Sun-dried-tomato pasta

Garlic warmed in olive oil, shredded basil, and Parmesan are all that's needed to turn this pasta into a splendid first course.

- 1½ cups unbleached flour
- ½ teaspoon coarse salt
- 2 sun-dried tomatoes, plus 1 teaspoon tomato oil from jar
- 1 large egg

To mix by hand: Combine flour and salt as directed for Pasta Gialla (opposite page). Mince tomatoes almost to a paste. Combine tomatoes and tomato oil with egg, then make a well in the center of the flour and add the egg-tomato mixture. Continue as directed for Pasta Gialla. *To mix in a food processor:* Put flour and salt in work bowl of processor fitted with the steel blade. Process 3 seconds to blend. Add tomatoes and process until they are blended. Add egg and tomato oil and continue as directed for Pasta Gialla.

Makes 1¼ pounds pasta.

SAUCES

The sauces suitable for pasta are as numerous and varied as the cook can imagine. However, a few basics should be mastered by anyone who wants to perfect a repertoire of pasta dishes. A northern-style cooked-tomato sauce, an uncooked tomato sauce, a tomato-meat sauce, a cream sauce, and pesto are not only useful on their own but also important building blocks for other dishes.

PESTO GENOVESE
Garlic and basil sauce with pine nuts

Pesto is a summer sauce, to make when basil is abundant and inexpensive. Its pungent aroma is unforgettable, whether it's tossed with hot linguine or stirred into a steaming minestrone. For Genoese sailors long at sea, a fragrant *pasta al pesto* is the traditional welcome home.

- 2 cups fresh basil leaves, loosely packed
- ½ cup light olive oil
- 2 tablespoons pine nuts, toasted
- 4 large cloves garlic, minced
- 1 teaspoon coarse salt
- ½ cup freshly grated Parmesan
- 2 tablespoons freshly grated Pecorino Romano cheese
- 3 tablespoons unsalted butter, softened

Put basil, olive oil, pine nuts, garlic, and salt in a blender or food processor. Blend or process until smooth. Transfer to a bowl and stir in Parmesan, Pecorino Romano, and butter.

Makes 1 cup.

Make-Ahead Tip Pesto may be made up to 1 week ahead, covered with a thin film of olive oil, and refrigerated in an airtight container. It may frozen for up to 1 month, covered with a thin film of olive oil. If you plan to freeze it, make Pesto without the garlic; stir minced garlic in just before using. Or freeze Pesto in ice-cube trays, then unmold and store cubes in plastic bag. Each cube will sauce one portion of pasta. In this case, wait to incorporate Parmesan, butter, and garlic until ready to serve.

SUGO DI POMODORO
Northern-style tomato sauce

Cooks in northern Italy often enrich sauces with butter. They add vegetables and herbs for depth, then simmer the sauce slowly to marry the flavors. Their basic tomato sauce is a building block for dozens of other dishes: lasagne, cannelloni, and ravioli; baked vegetable casseroles; and braised entrées. If you can't get sweet, vine-ripened tomatoes, use the best available canned variety.

- 2 teaspoons olive oil
- 4 teaspoons butter
- 1 large carrot, peeled and diced
- 2 ribs celery, diced
- 1 onion, diced
- 2 tablespoons minced garlic
- 1 teaspoon flour
- 3 pounds ripe tomatoes, peeled, seeded, and chopped, or one 28-ounce can plum tomatoes, whirled briefly in a blender
- 1 tablespoon tomato paste
  Pinch sugar
- ¼ cup fresh chopped basil or 1 teaspoon dried basil
- 4 sprigs fresh parsley
- 2 sprigs fresh oregano
- 1 bay leaf
  Salt and freshly ground black pepper

Heat oil and butter in a large, heavy saucepan over moderate heat. When butter foams, add carrot, celery, onion, and garlic and stew gently for 10 minutes. Stir in flour and continue cooking 5 minutes. Add tomatoes, tomato paste, sugar, basil, parsley, oregano, and bay leaf. Simmer, partly covered, for 1 hour. Remove bay leaf and herb stems. Pass sauce through a food mill if you prefer a smoother texture. Adjust seasoning to taste with salt and pepper.

Makes 4 cups.

Make-Ahead Tip Sauce may be made up to 1 week ahead and refrigerated. It may be frozen for up to 1 month.

SALSA DI CREMA E FORMAGGIO
Parmesan cream sauce

Use this delicate sauce from northern Italy to dress up almost any pasta, fresh or dried. Bathe fettuccine in it and you've made a classic Fettuccine Alfredo.

- 2 tablespoons olive oil
- 1 tablespoon butter
- 3 tablespoons minced shallots
- ½ cup heavy cream
- ½ cup freshly grated Parmesan

Heat olive oil and butter in a skillet over moderate heat. Add shallots; cook gently until soft. Add cream; cook over low heat 3 to 4 minutes more, whisking to incorporate cream. Add Parmesan and remove from heat.

Makes about 1 cup, 4 to 6 servings.

Make-Ahead Tip Sauce may be made up to 4 hours ahead and refrigerated. Reheat gently before serving.

SUGO DI POMODORI FRESCHI
Uncooked fresh-tomato and herb sauce

Only fresh, vine-ripened, height-of-season tomatoes will do for the uncooked sauce found throughout Italy. When hot pasta hits cool tomatoes and fresh herbs, the aroma explodes!

- 3 pounds fresh, ripe tomatoes, peeled, seeded, and diced (see page 29)
- 2 tablespoons garlic, finely minced
- ½ cup olive oil
- ¼ cup chopped fresh basil or 1 tablespoon minced fresh oregano
- 2 tablespoons minced fresh parsley
- ½ teaspoon hot red-pepper flakes
  Freshly ground black pepper, to taste
- 1 tablespoon balsamic vinegar
- 1 teaspoon coarse salt

Combine all ingredients but salt in a large nonaluminum bowl. Stir to blend well, then let sit at room temperature for 30 minutes. Just before serving, add salt.

Makes slightly over 2 cups, 4 servings.

RAGÙ BOLOGNESE
Classic Bolognese sauce

The cooking of Bologna is widely considered the richest in Italy. No dainty herbs and textures for the Bolognese: They add body to their tomato sauce with meat, lots of vegetables, and milk or cream. Bolognese sauce is especially good with sturdy pasta—like shells or rigatoni—that have holes or ridges to trap the sauce.

- ½ cup olive oil
- ½ cup unsalted butter
- 1½ cups diced onion
- 1 cup diced celery
- 1 cup peeled and diced carrot
- 2 pounds extra-lean ground beef
- 1¾ cups dry white wine
- 1 cup milk
- 5 pounds ripe tomatoes, peeled, seeded, and chopped (see page 29), or two 28-ounce cans plum tomatoes, whirled briefly in a blender
- 1 teaspoon coarse salt
- ⅛ teaspoon freshly grated nutmeg
- 1 teaspoon freshly ground black pepper

Heat oil and butter in a medium stockpot over moderate heat. When butter foams, add onions, celery, and carrots and cook for 10 minutes. Add beef, breaking it up with a wooden spoon; cook until meat is lightly browned. Add wine and simmer until wine has been completely absorbed. Add milk and simmer until milk has been completely absorbed. Add tomatoes, salt, nutmeg, and pepper and simmer gently, uncovered, until mixture is reduced to a rich sauce, about 2 hours and 30 minutes. Taste and adjust seasoning. Serve immediately over egg noodles or cool and refrigerate.

Makes about 4 cups.

Make-Ahead Tip Sauce may be made up to 1 week ahead and refrigerated. It may be frozen for up to 2 months.

PASTA FAVORITES, NORTH AND SOUTH

Italian pasta dishes differ from north to south. The rich, elaborate northern dishes are usually made with fresh pasta and often contain butter, meat, and cream. Lasagne con Sugo di Funghi Secchi and Cannelloni are typical of the north.

In the south, dried pasta takes the place of fresh, and the dishes become simpler and more aggressively seasoned. Along the southern coasts, fish and shellfish appear frequently. Maccheroni al Tonno bears a distinctly southern stamp.

The following recipes give just a brief glimpse of this vast repertoire.

SPAGHETTI CON AGLIO E OLIO
Spaghetti with garlic and oil

A straightforward garlic-and-oil sauce (found throughout Italy) is delightful when made with young garlic. Choose heads with firm, pale ivory cloves that have a fresh, sweet flavor. Cloves that are sprouting or hot and bitter will ruin the dish.

1 large head young garlic
½ cup olive oil
1 tablespoon unsalted butter
1 pound dried spaghetti
   Pinch hot red-pepper flakes
   (optional)
2 tablespoons minced anchovies
   (optional)
   Salt and freshly ground
   black pepper

1. Separate head of garlic into cloves. Peel and chop cloves. Heat oil and butter in a skillet over moderate heat. Add garlic and sauté until fragrant. Remove from heat and let stand 20 minutes.

2. Cook spaghetti in plenty of boiling salted water until just done. Drain thoroughly, then transfer to a warm serving bowl. Reheat garlic and oil mixture, stirring in pepper flakes or anchovies (if used). Add sauce to pasta and toss well. Season to taste with salt and pepper. Serve immediately.

Serves 4 generously.

A robust Sugo di Pomodoro—a basic tomato sauce—is important to countless Italian dishes, from lasagne and cannelloni to braised meats and vegetables.

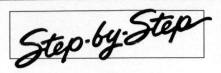

MAKING TORTELLINI

Tortellini can be made with a variety of fillings. In the photographs here the Pumpkin Filling from the recipe at right is used.

The pasta should be quite thin. For greatest ease of preparation, use a pasta machine.

Once cooked, tortellini may be added to beef or chicken broth, as in Tortellini in Brodo, at right. They may also be simply sauced with butter or bathed in a sauce of butter, cream, and cheese (see Salsa di Crema e Formaggio, page 36).

Tortellini can be formed a few hours ahead and spread on lightly floured baking sheets. Make sure they do not touch. Cover and refrigerate.

Tortellini can also be frozen before cooking. Follow directions for freezing ravioli on page 43.

2. *Fold circle in half to enclose filling; press edges together firmly to seal.*

3. *With sealed edge out, place folded circle over index finger. Bring ends toward each other under the finger, turning sealed outer edge up to form a cuff.*

1. *Cut 2-inch circles from pasta dough. Put a scant teaspoon of filling in center of each. Brush edges lightly with cold water.*

4. *Pinch ends together firmly. Let tortellini dry for a few minutes on a lightly floured surface before cooking.*

TORTELLINI IN BRODO
Tortellini in broth

It is said that tortellini are the inspiration of a lovesick cook, who shaped them to resemble the navel of his beloved. Conjectures aside, they're delicious in soup and are commonly served that way as a first course in Italy. They are often stuffed with ground veal and prosciutto, but the Modenese pumpkin filling below is popular, too. Use them in soups, as in this recipe, or toss them with butter and serve them with your Thanksgiving turkey.

> 2 recipes Pasta Gialla or other
>   pasta dough (see pages
>   34–35) or 1 recipe each of two
>   different kinds
> 6 cups chicken stock, preferably
>   homemade

Pumpkin Filling

> ½ cup cooked, puréed pumpkin
>   or winter squash
> 5 ounces freshly grated
>   Parmesan
> ¼ cup ricotta
> 2 eggs plus 1 egg yolk
> 1 tablespoon brandy
> 1 teaspoon powdered sage
>   Salt and freshly ground
>   black pepper
>   Pinch nutmeg

1. Make filling.

2. Roll out pasta and form tortellini as shown at left, using a teaspoon of filling for each one. You will have 36 to 40 tortellini. Bring stock to a boil in a saucepan. Add tortellini. They will sink, then float. After they float to the surface, cook 2 minutes. Remove one and taste for doneness. Transfer tortellini as they are cooked to warm soup plates. Ladle hot chicken stock over each portion.

Serves 5 or 6.

Pumpkin Filling Combine pumpkin, Parmesan, ricotta, eggs, egg yolk, brandy, and sage in a bowl. Season to taste with salt, pepper, and nutmeg.

CANNELLONI
Stuffed pasta rolls

Made from neat rectangles of pasta rolled around a savory filling, cannelloni can be a main course or, in small portions, a first course. In this dish from Abruzzi, both herb and egg doughs are filled with a spinach-and-cheese mixture, then topped with a creamy *balsamella* and a meaty Bolognese sauce.

- 1 recipe Pasta Gialla
  (see page 34)
- 1 recipe Pasta di Herbe
  (see page 35)
- 1 recipe Salsa Balsamella
  (see page 42)
- 1 recipe Ragù Bolognese
  (see page 36)
- ¼ cup freshly grated Parmesan
- 3 tablespoons unsalted butter,
  at room temperature

Spinach and Cheese Filling

- 2 tablespoons olive oil
- 2 tablespoons minced shallot
- 2 tablespoons minced carrot
- 4 bunches fresh spinach,
  stemmed, leaves blanched,
  squeezed dry, and chopped
- ⅓ pound prosciutto, sliced
  paper-thin and shredded
- ¾ pound whole-milk ricotta
- 1 cup freshly grated Parmesan
- ¼ cup grated mozzarella
- 2 eggs plus 1 egg yolk
  Salt and freshly ground
  black pepper
  Pinch nutmeg

1. Roll pasta into sheets. Cut into 16 rectangles approximately 3 by 4 inches. Bring a large pot of salted water to a boil. Parboil pasta in batches for 10 seconds. Remove with a slotted spoon and refresh under ice water. Drain and dry thoroughly. Arrange atop clean dish towels. Top with clean dish towels and set aside.

2. Preheat oven to 350° F. Spoon 3 tablespoons of filling on each pasta rectangle. Roll up into a neat tube. Spread 1 cup of Salsa Balsamella over bottom of an ovenproof casserole, approximately 11 by 14 inches. Arrange cannelloni in the casserole side by side, alternating egg and herb rolls. Top with Ragù Bolognese and remaining Balsamella. Dust with Parmesan, dot with butter, cover with foil, and bake 10 minutes. Uncover; bake 10 minutes more to brown the top. Serve immediately.

Serves 8 as a main course, 16 as a first course.

Spinach and Cheese Filling Heat olive oil in a large skillet over moderate heat. Add shallot and carrot; sauté 3 minutes. Remove from heat. Stir in spinach, prosciutto, ricotta, Parmesan, mozzarella, eggs, and egg yolk. Season to taste with salt, pepper, and nutmeg.

PASTA PUTTANESCA
Harlot's pasta

Legend has it that we owe this dish to Rome's "ladies of the night," who favored it because it was so quickly made. It's a spicy, sassy dish that calls for lots of crisp white wine.

- ¼ cup plus 1 tablespoon olive oil
- 2 tablespoons butter
- ½ cup minced onion
- 2 tablespoons minced garlic
- 2½ cups peeled, seeded,
  and chopped tomatoes
- 2 ounces anchovies, minced
- ½ teaspoon hot red-pepper flakes
- 1 tablespoon capers
- 1 cup unpitted Calamata olives
- ¼ cup julienned prosciutto
  (optional)
- 1 pound dried spaghetti
- 2 tablespoons minced parsley

1. Heat ¼ cup olive oil and the butter in a large skillet over low heat. When butter foams, add onion and garlic; sauté slowly until very soft, about 10 minutes. Add tomatoes; simmer 10 minutes. Add anchovies and pepper flakes; cook 1 minute. Stir in capers, olives, and prosciutto (if used).

2. Bring a large pot of salted water to a boil. Add remaining tablespoon olive oil and spaghetti and cook until pasta is just tender. Drain thoroughly and add to sauce in skillet. Toss together well and serve immediately, garnished with minced parsley.

Serves 4.

MACCHERONI AL TONNO
Pasta with fresh tuna

This brassy Sicilian sauce is not for delicate palates. Garlic, anchovies, capers, and olives enliven its fresh-tomato base; strips of tuna are tossed in at the last minute. This is a summer dish, to precede grilled fish or grilled shrimp.

- 4 cup fresh bread crumbs
- ¼ cup minced parsley
- ¼ cup freshly grated Romano
- 8 ounces fresh tuna fillet,
  cut into strips approximately
  ¼ by ¼ by 2½ inches long
  Freshly ground black pepper
- 3 tablespoons olive oil
- ½ cup minced yellow onion
- 1 tablespoon minced garlic
- 3 anchovy fillets, minced
- 1 pound plum tomatoes, peeled,
  seeded, and chopped
- 1 tablespoon capers
- ¼ cup pitted green olives
- 1 pound dried elbow-shaped
  macaroni

1. Combine bread crumbs, parsley, and cheese in a small bowl. Set aside. Season tuna lightly with pepper.

2. Heat olive oil in a large skillet over moderate heat. Add onion and garlic and sauté 3 minutes. Add anchovies and mash them with a wooden spoon until they "melt" into the garlic and onions. Add tomatoes. Cover partially and simmer 15 minutes. Turn heat to medium-high, add tuna, and toss quickly, cooking just until tuna is barely done. Stir in capers and olives, cook 30 seconds, cover, and remove from heat. Taste and adjust seasoning as necessary.

3. Bring a large pot of salted water to a boil. Add pasta and cook until just tender. Drain thoroughly and transfer to a warm serving bowl. Add half the bread-crumb mixture and toss well. Ladle the sauce over the top, then garnish with the remaining bread-crumb mixture.

Serves 4.

A bouquet of spring vegetables makes Pasta Primavera one of the lightest and liveliest Italian pasta dishes.

FETTUCCINE CON COZZE
Fettuccine with mussels and greens

The nutty-flavored green that Italians call arugula (also known as rocket or roquette) works particularly well in this Neapolitan dish, but other greens may be substituted. Take care not to overcook the mussels; the greens should be just barely wilted.

  ¼ *cup olive oil*
  ¼ *cup minced onion*
  2 *tablespoons minced garlic*
  ½ *cup dry white wine*
  1 *tablespoon grated lemon rind*
  1 *sweet red pepper, diced*
  6 *pounds fresh mussels, scrubbed clean and debearded (see page 67)*
  1 *tablespoon grappa (optional)*
  1 *pound fresh spinach, stems removed, leaves washed and dried*
2½ *cups loosely packed arugula or other bitter greens (watercress, dandelion greens, collard greens, turnip greens)*
  1 *pound homemade fettuccine (use Pasta Gialla, page 34, or Pasta di Herbe, page 35) Freshly ground black pepper*

1. Heat olive oil in a large saucepan over medium heat. Add onion and garlic and sauté slowly until soft, about 3 to 5 minutes. Add wine, lemon rind, and red pepper; raise heat to high and add mussels. Cover and steam mussels until they open, about 3 minutes. Lift the lid and check them occasionally, removing those mussels that have opened. Discard any that refuse to open. Remove all mussels to a warm bowl. If you wish, add grappa to pan and flame; when flames die down, add spinach and greens. Or just add spinach and greens to still-hot pan. Cook greens about 10 seconds, until they are just wilted. Remove from heat.

2. Bring a large pot of salted water to a boil. Add pasta and cook until just done. Drain noodles well and transfer to pan with sauce. Return pan to low heat and toss noodles to coat well with sauce. Add mussels and toss again, then divide pasta among warm serving plates. Top each portion with freshly ground black pepper and serve immediately.

Serves 4.

PASTA PRIMAVERA
Spring vegetable pasta

The typical *pasta primavera* is a veritable garden on a plate—the most tender young vegetables tossed with herbs and thin pasta. You can readily substitute whatever is freshest in your market, but remember to aim for lively colors and contrasting textures. This is a Bolognese recipe.

> 1 pound sugar snap peas, strings removed, or *1 cup shelled fresh peas*
> 1 pound fresh asparagus
> 1 cup sliced slender green beans, in 2-inch lengths
> ½ cup thin carrot strips
> 3 tablespoons olive oil plus 1 tablespoon if using dried pasta
> 2 tablespoons unsalted butter
> ½ cup diced sweet red pepper
> ½ cup diced sweet yellow pepper (optional)
> 2 tablespoons pine nuts, toasted
> 1 recipe Pasta di Herbe (see page 35) or ¾ pound dried spaghettini or cappelletti pasta
> 1 cup thinly shredded romaine lettuce
> 2 tablespoons minced fresh chives
> Salt
> 4 tablespoons minced fresh parsley, for garnish
> Freshly grated Parmesan

1. Bring a large pot of salted water to a boil. Blanch peas, asparagus, beans, and carrots separately, removing each batch to ice water as it is crisp but still tender, to stop the cooking. Drain well and pat dry. Save the cooking water.

2. Heat the 3 tablespoons olive oil and the butter in a large, heavy skillet over moderate heat. When butter foams, add red and yellow peppers (if used) and sauté one minute. Add pine nuts and sauté one more minute. Add blanched and dried peas, asparagus, beans, and carrots and toss until coated with oil and warmed through.

3. To cook pasta, bring the reserved vegetable water to a rolling boil. If you are using dried pasta, add 1 tablespoon oil; if you are using fresh pasta, there is no need to add oil. Add pasta and cook until just done. Drain well and transfer to a warm serving bowl. Add hot vegetables to pasta with romaine and chives. Toss well, add salt to taste, then toss again. Divide pasta among warm serving plates. Garnish each portion with minced parsley and pass grated Parmesan separately.

Serves 4.

FETTUCCINE CARBONARA
Pasta with bacon and eggs

In this popular Roman dish, the heat of the pasta cooks the eggs to yield a sauce made right in the serving bowl. Carbonara is a rich first course; follow it with a simple veal or chicken dish.

> 2 tablespoons olive oil
> 1 tablespoon unsalted butter
> 2 tablespoons finely minced garlic
> 8 ounces pancetta, in small dice
> ⅓ cup dry white wine
> 2 large eggs
> ⅓ cup freshly grated Pecorino Romano cheese
> ⅓ cup freshly grated Parmesan
> 1 recipe Pasta Gialla (see page 34)
> Salt and freshly ground black pepper, to taste

1. Heat oil and butter in a skillet over moderate heat. When butter foams, add garlic and sauté until garlic is fragrant. Add pancetta and fry until it is lightly browned. Add wine and simmer until wine is almost completely evaporated. Remove skillet from heat.

2. Break eggs into a large serving bowl and beat lightly. Stir in Pecorino Romano and Parmesan.

3. Cook pasta in plenty of boiling salted water until just done. Drain thoroughly; add to egg-cheese mixture. Toss well, then add hot pancetta mixture and toss again. Season with salt and plenty of pepper.

Serves 4.

PAPPARDELLE CON PESTO E PATATE
Broad noodles with pesto and potatoes

If you order pasta with pesto along the Italian Ligurian coast, you'll probably spot potato slices among the noodles. To Americans unaccustomed to starch-upon-starch, the combination surprises, but the first taste invariably wins converts. A crisp Italian Orvieto or Frascati is a fine accompaniment.

> 1 pound new red potatoes, scrubbed
> 2 tablespoons olive oil, plus 1 tablespoon if using dried pasta
> 1 tablespoon coarse salt
> 1 recipe Pasta Gialla (see page 34) or 1 pound broad noodles, storebought
> 1 recipe Pesto Genovese (see page 35), at room temperature
> 2 tablespoons toasted pine nuts, for garnish
> 2 tablespoons minced parsley, for garnish
> Freshly grated Parmesan

1. In a vegetable steamer, steam potatoes until just tender. Dry well, slice ¼ inch thick, then toss in a bowl with the 2 tablespoons olive oil and the salt.

2. Bring a large pot of salted water to a boil. If you are using dried pasta, add 1 tablespoon oil. Add pasta and cook until just done. Drain well and transfer to a warm serving bowl. Add potatoes and pesto and toss thoroughly, making sure that potatoes are coated with pesto, too. Garnish with pine nuts and parsley. Divide pasta among warm serving plates and pass the Parmesan separately.

Serves 4.

RAVIOLI DI SCAROLE E FORMAGGI
Spinach ravioli stuffed with cheese and escarole

These plump little pillows from Bologna have an unusual savory filling that's complemented by either tomato sauce or a light Salsa di Crema e Formaggio. They're quite rich and should be followed with a simple main course.

- 2 recipes Pasta Verde (see page 34)
- 1 recipe Sugo di Pomodoro or 1 recipe Salsa di Crema e Formaggio (both, page 36)
- 3 tablespoons minced parsley, for garnish
- ¼ cup freshly grated Parmesan, for garnish

Cheese and Escarole Filling

- 3 tablespoons olive oil
- 1 tablespoon butter
- 3 tablespoons minced leek or onion
- ½ tablespoon minced garlic
- 1 large bunch escarole, washed and finely shredded
- 1 teaspooon dried oregano
- 2 tablespoons Marsala
- 2 tablespoons whipping cream
- ¼ cup whole-milk ricotta
- ¼ cup grated Bel Paese or grated fresh mozzarella
  Salt and freshly ground black pepper
  Pinch nutmeg

1. Roll pasta dough out into sheets. Place ¾ teaspoon filling at regular intervals the length of the pasta (opposite page). Place another sheet of pasta over the first and use your fingers to press sheets together between the mounds of filling. Cut ravioli with a pizza cutter or pastry wheel. Use a fork to crimp the edges.

2. Bring a large pot of salted water to a boil. Add ravioli to boiling water a few at a time; do not crowd the pot.

Ravioli will sink, then float. After they begin to float, cook 2½ minutes. Remove one and taste for doneness. With a slotted spoon, remove cooked ravioli to a warm platter and keep warm in a low oven. Add remaining ravioli to boiling water in batches until all are cooked.

3. Meanwhile, reheat sauce. When all ravioli are on the platter, top with hot sauce. Garnish with parsley and Parmesan.

Serves 4 to 6.

Cheese and Escarole Filling Heat oil and butter in a skillet over moderate heat. When butter foams, add leek and garlic. Sauté gently until leek is very soft, about 15 minutes. Add escarole and oregano and sauté 2 minutes. Add Marsala, turn heat up to high, and cook until Marsala is almost completely evaporated. Reduce heat to medium and add cream. Stir to combine; simmer until cream thickens into a sauce, about 2 to 3 minutes. Remove from heat and cool slightly. Stir in cheeses; season to taste with salt, pepper, and nutmeg.

LASAGNE CON SUGO DI FUNGHI SECCHI
Lasagne with dried-mushroom sauce

The dried Italian mushrooms called *porcini* add a rich, woodsy flavor to any sauce or dish. Here they lend their fragrance to a rustic meatless lasagne from Piedmont (substitute water for the chicken stock if you prefer a vegetarian version). Serve it in cool weather as a main course with a salad, or in small portions as a first course followed by a chicken or veal roast.

- 1½ recipes Pasta Gialla (see page 34) or Pasta di Herbe (see page 35) or 1 pound dried lasagne noodles
  Olive oil
- 1 cup ricotta
- ½ cup minced parsley plus 3 tablespoons, for garnish
- ¼ cup freshly grated Parmesan

Sugo di Funghi Secchi

- 1 cup chicken stock
- 2 ounces dried porcini mushrooms
- 3 tablespoons olive oil
- 1 tablespoon butter
- 1 onion, minced
- 2 tablespoons finely minced garlic
- 2¾ cups tomato sauce (preferably Sugo di Pomodoro, page 36, but storebought will do) or puréed and strained fresh tomatoes
  Grated rind of 1 lemon
- ½ cup small fresh basil leaves, loosely packed
- 2 sprigs fresh oregano
- ¼ cup parsley sprigs
- 1 bay leaf
- 1¼ cups dry red wine
  Salt and freshly ground black pepper
- 3 tablespoons shredded basil

Salsa Balsamella

- 6 tablespoons unsalted butter
- 1½ tablespoons flour
- 3 cups milk
- ⅓ to ½ cup half-and-half
- 1 tablespoon sweet vermouth
  Pinch nutmeg
  Salt and white pepper

1. If you are using fresh pasta, roll out dough and cut it into lasagne shape (see page 7). Bring a large pot of salted water to a boil. Add lasagne noodles and cook until almost tender. Drain and refresh under cold water. Drain thoroughly and dry. Moisten noodles with olive oil and spread out on clean kitchen towels.

2. Preheat oven to 350° F. Coat bottom and sides of a casserole pan (approximately 13 by 11 by 2 inches) with 2 tablespoons olive oil. Spread 1 cup Sugo di Funghi Secchi over the bottom of the pan. Top with a layer of one third of the lasagne noodles. Combine ricotta, ½ cup minced parsley, and half of the Salsa Balsamella. Spread this mixture over the noodle layer. Top with another layer of one third of the noodles, then 1½ cups of the mushroom sauce, the remaining balsamella, a final layer of noodles, and the remaining mushroom sauce. Dust the top with Parmesan.

3. Cover pan with foil and bake 15 minutes. Uncover and bake until lasagne bubbles around the edges. Do not overcook. Let rest 10 minutes before serving.

Serves 6.

Sugo di Funghi Secchi

1. In a small saucepan bring stock to a boil. Add dried mushrooms and simmer 20 minutes. Carefully lift mushrooms out with a slotted spoon. Strain liquid through cheesecloth and reserve. Pick through porcini carefully to remove any grit. Chop coarsely.

2. Heat oil and butter in a large skillet over moderate heat. When butter foams, add onion and sauté 3 minutes. Add garlic and sauté until onion softens and begins to color, an additional 5 to 7 minutes. Add tomato sauce, lemon rind, basil leaves, oregano, parsley, and bay leaf. Stir well, then add strained stock, mushrooms, wine, and salt and pepper to taste. Simmer until liquid is reduced to a rich, dark sauce, about 45 to 50 minutes. Remove bay leaf and herb sprigs. Taste and adjust seasoning. Stir in shredded basil and remove from heat.

Makes about 4 cups.

Salsa Balsamella In a 1½-quart saucepan over moderate heat, melt 4 tablespoons of the butter. Add flour and cook, stirring, for 5 minutes. Gradually add milk in a slow, steady stream, whisking constantly. Cook over medium heat 20 minutes, stirring occasionally. Stir in ⅓ cup of the half-and-half, vermouth, nutmeg, and salt and pepper to taste. Continue cooking about 15 minutes, or until sauce is thick and smooth. If sauce thickens too much, add a little more half-and-half. Whisk in remaining butter. Taste and adjust seasoning. Set aside to cool.

Makes about 3 cups.

PREPARING RAVIOLI

Ravioli can be made with a variety of fillings. In the photographs here, Pasta Verde (spinach pasta) is used with a filling of escarole and cheese (see recipe on facing page). You could also use the pumpkin filling from the recipe for Tortellini in Brodo, page 38, or the spinach and cheese filling from the recipe for Cannelloni, page 39. Other pasta doughs can also be used. See pages 34 and 35 for Pasta Gialla (basic egg dough) and its variations. Be careful to match the dough and filling to make a compatible combination.

The pasta dough should be quite thin. For greatest ease of preparation, use a pasta machine.

Once they have been cooked, ravioli can be added to beef or chicken broth. They can also be sauced with Sugo di Pomodori Freschi (see page 36) or Salsa di Crema e Formaggio (see page 36).

Ravioli can be prepared a few hours ahead of serving time and spread on lightly floured baking sheets. Make sure they do not touch. Cover and refrigerate.

Ravioli can also be frozen after they have been formed (and before cooking). Arrange ravioli in a single layer on a baking sheet or tray, being sure they are not touching. Place tray in freezer. When ravioli are frozen solid, remove them from tray and place in a freezer-weight plastic bag or other freezer container. They can be stored in the freezer up to three months.

1. *Roll pasta dough into sheets. Place mounds of filling, about ¾ teaspoon each, at regular intervals the length of the pasta. Brush lightly with cold water between the mounds.*

2. *Place another sheet of pasta over the first and use your fingers to press sheets together between the mounds of filling.*

3. *Cut ravioli with a pizza cutter or pastry wheel. Use a fork to crimp and seal the edges.*

A SICILIAN COUNTRY DINNER

Pomodori dell' Estate
(see page 109)

Minestra all' Aglio

Baccalà Fritto alla Siciliana

Focaccia
(see page 52)

Caciocavallo
(see page 20)

Mele ed Uve
(Apples and Grapes)

Dolci della Festa

This menu is sensible for company because so much of the meal may be made ahead. Assemble the tomato casserole in the morning, bake it just before guests arrive, and serve it at room temperature. The soup, too, may be made in the morning, except for the final addition of cheese. The sauce for the salt cod is made ahead, but the fish is fried at the last minute. The Focaccia can be made in the morning and warmed through before serving; offer it along with the first two courses. Drink a crisp Italian white wine throughout the dinner, and pour espresso or strong coffee with the party cookies.

MINESTRA ALL' AGLIO
Chicken broth with garlic

Potatoes, cheese, and cream enrich this quickly made chicken soup. A healthy dose of garlic and hot red-pepper flakes brand it as Sicilian.

> 5 cups chicken stock
> 1 cup peeled and diced raw potato
> 3 tablespoons olive oil
> ¼ cup sliced garlic
> ½ cup minced onion
> ½ cup whipping cream
> ½ cup milk
> ½ teaspoon hot red-pepper flakes
> 2 ounces fontina, grated
> Coarse salt

1. Combine stock and potato in a large saucepan. Bring to a boil over high heat, reduce heat to maintain a simmer, and cook 10 minutes.

2. While stock is simmering heat olive oil in a large saucepan over moderately low heat. Add garlic and onion and sauté gently for 10 minutes; do not let garlic and onion brown. Add stock and potato and simmer 20 minutes, covered. Transfer mixture to a blender in batches along with cream, milk, and red-pepper flakes. Blend until smooth.

3. Put mixture in a clean large saucepan. Add 2 tablespoons of the fontina and reheat, stirring until cheese melts and mixture is almost boiling. Add salt to taste. Serve immediately, garnishing each portion with some of the remaining fontina.

Serves 4.

Make-Ahead Tip The soup may be made through step 2 several hours ahead and refrigerated.

BACCALÀ FRITTO ALLA SICILIANA
Fried salt cod Sicilian style

A day-long soaking rids dried salt cod of its excess salt and restores its meaty, firm texture. Briefly marinated with lemon juice and hot red-pepper flakes, then breaded and deep-fried, it is as sweet and succulent as any fresh-caught fish. Serve it as the Sicilians do, with a pungent olive-and-anchovy sauce, and accompany it with a bone-dry Verdicchio or Sicilian Corvo. Note that the sauce must stand for at least 12 hours and can be made as much as a week in advance.

> 1½ pounds boneless salt cod
> 2 cups milk
> ¼ cup olive oil
> ¼ cup lemon juice
> 2 tablespoons minced parsley
> ½ onion, minced
> ½ teaspoon hot red-pepper flakes
> Flour, for dredging
> ¼ cup dry white wine
> 2 eggs
> 2 cups soft bread crumbs
> 2 tablespoons corn oil

Olive Sauce

> 1½ cups green pimiento-stuffed olives
> ⅔ cup olive oil
> ½ cup minced parsley
> 1 sweet red bell pepper, seeded, with ribs removed, and minced
> 1½ ounces anchovy fillets, mashed
> ¼ cup capers
> 1 tablespoon minced garlic
> 1 tablespoon minced fresh oregano
> 1 teaspoon black pepper

1. Put salt cod in a baking dish and cover with cold water. Refrigerate 24 hours, changing the water 3 times. On the final change, add the milk to the water.

2. Drain salt cod and pat dry. Cut into 12 pieces. In a large bowl, combine olive oil, lemon juice, parsley, onion, and red-pepper flakes. Put fish pieces in the bowl and marinate 45 minutes at room temperature.

3. Put flour on a plate or a sheet of waxed paper. Combine wine and egg in a small bowl; whisk to blend. Have bread crumbs ready on a plate. Drain fish. Dredge each piece lightly in flour. Dip fish in egg mixture, letting excess drip off, then coat with bread crumbs. Transfer breaded salt cod to a plate or baking sheet.

4. Heat corn oil in a large skillet over moderately high heat. Fry fish on both sides until nicely browned, about 3 to 4 minutes on each side depending on thickness. Drain on paper towels and arrange on a warm serving platter. Spoon Olive Sauce over cod and serve immediately.

Serves 4.

Olive Sauce Chop olives coarsely. Put in a ceramic, stainless steel, or glass bowl along with olive oil, parsley, bell pepper, anchovies, capers, garlic, oregano, and black pepper. Stir to blend. Cover and refrigerate for at least 12 hours or up to 1 week. Serve at room temperature.

DOLCI DELLA FESTA
Party cookies

These chocolate macaroons are traditionally eaten at All Souls' Day parties.

> 2 egg whites
> ½ cup sugar
>   Pinch of salt
> 6 ounces milk chocolate, melted
> 2 teaspoons vanilla extract
> ½ teaspoon ground cinnamon
> 1 cup unsweetened shredded coconut

1. Preheat oven to 325° F. Beat egg whites until frothy. Add sugar and salt and beat until stiff but not dry.

2. In a medium bowl combine chocolate, vanilla, cinnamon, and coconut. Gently fold in egg whites.

3. Drop batter by teaspoons onto a lightly greased baking sheet. Bake 15 minutes. Cool on a rack and store in airtight containers (cookies can be stored for 2 to 3 weeks).

Makes 3 dozen cookies.

This country dinner reflects the Sicilian taste for bold flavors: garlic and peppers, anchovies and capers. There is nothing refined about dishes like Minestra all' Aglio or Baccalà Fritto alla Siciliana. They are the creations of good home cooks: The presentations are simple; the flavors, direct. The soup and fish are accompanied by a tomato casserole and crusty Focaccia; fresh fruit and cookies complete the meal.

Starting with corn, rice, and wheat, Italian cooks make such favorite foods as polenta, risotto, a multitude of breads, and pizzas by the dozen.

Breads, Pizza & Grains

Many of the earthy basics of Italian cooking are presented in this chapter. Virtually every meal includes bread, whether a sweet slice for breakfast (see Pane di Mattina alla Siciliana, page 50), a savory accompaniment to a soup lunch (see Pane per la Zuppa, page 49), or a crusty loaf with dinner (see Pane Toscano, page 48). In the north polenta (see page 58) and risotto (see page 61) are age-old traditions; from the south comes the much-beloved pizza (see page 53). A special feature of the chapter is a Pizza Party menu (see page 55).

Like French toast, Pane per la Zuppa is dipped in egg and then cooked to a golden finish. This Italian version, however, is savory—seasoned with garlic, fennel, and pepper and dusted with Parmesan—and it's baked. Serve Pane per la Zuppa with soup for a filling lunch or light dinner.

BREADS, PIZZA & GRAINS

Whole grains and grain derivatives are a large part of the Italian diet. Indeed, corn and rice in the north and wheat in the south are the foundation of many of Italy's best-known dishes. Corn is made into polenta (see page 58) and a variety of corn breads; short-grain rice becomes creamy risotto (see page 61); wheat, of course, is the basis of Italy's huge repertoire of breads, ranging from Pane Toscano (at right) to Focaccia (see page 52) to pizza (see page 53).

The beauty of pizza, breads, and grains is their versatility. Master the basic techniques, and then let your imagination and the state of your larder suggest variations. The recipes that follow merely hint at the enormous range of Italian pizzas, breads, and grains.

BREADS

The most basic sort of bread—nothing but flour, yeast, and water—plays a fundamental role in the Italian diet. In fact, many Italians consider good bread, good oil, and salt, and perhaps a vine-ripened tomato, enough to make them perfectly happy at lunch. But more often the basic bread is used to soak up juices from other dishes or to accompany Italy's famous cheeses (see page 20).

More elaborate breads play other roles. The sweet Pane di Mattina alla Siciliana (see page 50) is a foil for the bitter morning espresso. Pane Rustico (see page 50), packed with pancetta and cheese, is a perfect picnic bread, and Focaccia and Merenda Fiorentina (see page 49) are popular snacks. And a Focaccia di Palermo stuffed with sausage and cheese (see page 53) or a bubbling Pizza del Norte made with fontina and provolone (see page 53) can be enjoyed as a meal in itself.

Although most Italians buy their breads from the local *panetteria* (bakery), there is no denying the appeal of a homemade loaf. The interested home baker will want to try the following recipes and should find the results immensely satisfying.

PANE TOSCANO
Basic Tuscan bread

This rustic bread requires some patience but little actual working time. Begin the Starter four days ahead and you'll get a chewy, full-flavored loaf that is absolutely authentic. Its basic goodness is the perfect foil for antipasti, salads, soups, cheeses, and sauces of all sorts. Such wonderful bread can become an antipasto or a lunch in minutes: Just toast and rub with garlic, brush well with extravirgin olive oil, sprinkle with coarse salt, and top it with a crushed ripe tomato.

> 2 cups warm (105° F) water
> 6 cups (approximately) unbleached flour
> 1 teaspoon active dry yeast

Starter

- 1½ cups unbleached flour
- 1 teaspoon sugar
- ½ cup warm (105° F) water

1. Put half the Starter in a bowl; cover with cool water and soak 3 hours. Gently pour off the water, taking care not to lose any moist bits of dough at the bottom of the bowl. Add ½ cup of the warm water and 1 cup flour. Stir well, then cover and set aside for 3 hours. Add remaining warm water and as much of the remaining flour as necessary to make a dough firm enough to knead.

2. Turn out dough onto a lightly floured board and knead 15 minutes, adding more flour as necessary to make a firm, smooth dough. Form dough into 2 round loaves and place on a lightly oiled baking sheet. Snip tops of loaves with scissors at 2-inch intervals. Cover and let rise until doubled in bulk, about 2 hours.

3. When dough has almost doubled, preheat oven to 450° F and place a pan of hot water on the lowest rack. Bake bread 12 minutes at 450° F, then reduce heat to 375° F and continue baking until bread sounds hollow when tapped. Cool on racks before slicing.

Makes two 1-pound loaves.

Starter Combine flour, sugar, and the water in a bowl and mix to form a rough ball. Dough will be stiff and coarse. Dust with a little additional flour, cover, and set aside 4 days. Starter will become quite hard. On the fourth day, divide starter in half. Put half in a bowl covered with plastic wrap, at room temperature, to make dough; wrap remaining half and refrigerate it for up to 2 months.

Makes enough starter for 4 loaves.

MERENDA FIORENTINA
Florentine snack bread

This flat "pizza" bread is scented with rosemary, oil, and garlic, which fill the house with tantalizing aromas when it's baked. Cut it into "fingers" and serve it as a snack with a glass of red wine, or tuck it into your picnic basket along with roast chicken and Roasted Red Peppers (see page 14).

- 1 package active dry yeast
- 1 teaspoon salt
- 3 cups unbleached flour
- 1 cup warm (105° F) water
- 3 tablespoons olive oil plus olive oil for brushing crust
- 1 tablespoon minced garlic
  Cornmeal, for dusting
  Coarse salt
- 1 teaspoon minced fresh rosemary (optional)

1. Combine yeast, salt, and flour in a large bowl. Combine the water and oil in a small bowl. Add liquid to dry ingredients and mix until they form a rough mass. Knead mixture in the bowl with your hands until it holds together, then turn it out onto a lightly floured surface and knead in the garlic. Continue kneading until dough is smooth and elastic, about 8 minutes. Form into a ball and let rest on a lightly floured surface, covered, for 1 hour.

2. Preheat oven to 375° F. Roll dough into a 12- by 14-inch rectangle and transfer to a baking sheet sprinkled with cornmeal. Use your fingertips to make indentations in the dough at 2-inch intervals. Sprinkle dough lightly with coarse salt and drizzle olive oil over the top. Sprinkle with rosemary (if used). Bake until golden, about 25 minutes. Remove from the oven and brush with a little more olive oil. Cool slightly on a rack; serve warm.

Makes one 12- by 14-inch rectangle.

PANE PER LA ZUPPA
Bread for soup

This Neapolitan version of French toast is an excellent complement to a soup or stew. Thick slices of egg-dipped bread are seasoned with garlic, pepper, and fennel, then topped with Parmesan and baked until golden.

- 1 teaspoon minced garlic
- 1 tablespoon fennel seed, lightly crushed in a mortar
- 1 tablespoon freshly ground black pepper
- 1 teaspoon salt
- 5 or 6 eggs
- 3 or 4 tablespoons olive oil
- 1 loaf Pane Toscano (opposite page), cut in ¾-inch slices
- 2 tablespoons freshly grated Parmesan

1. Preheat oven to 350° F. Lightly oil a large baking sheet. Combine garlic, fennel seed, pepper, and salt in a small bowl and set aside.

2. Whisk together 5 eggs and 3 tablespoons olive oil. Dip bread slices in egg mixture one at a time and let them soak briefly to absorb some egg. Arrange bread slices on baking sheet. If bread is slightly stale, you may need an additional egg and a little extra oil.

3. Dust bread slices with half the fennel mixture. Bake 10 minutes. Turn slices, dust with remaining fennel mixture, and bake 10 minutes. Sprinkle with Parmesan and bake an additional 5 minutes or until bread is golden. Serve hot with soup or stew.

Makes 12 slices.

PANE RUSTICO
Country bacon-and-cheese bread

These round Roman loaves are practically a lunch in themselves, especially with a green salad and a bottle of red wine. They make delicious toast to accompany a chicken broth or a tomato soup, and when toasted and properly filled, they make the ultimate BLT.

    2 packages active dry yeast
    2 cups warm (105° F) water
    4½ cups (approximately)
       unbleached flour
    ½ cup whole wheat flour
    1 tablespoon coarse salt
    ½ cup coarse cornmeal
    4 ounces pancetta, sliced thin
    8 ounces whole-milk mozza-
       rella, cut in ⅓-inch cubes
       Cornmeal, for dusting

1. Combine yeast and ½ cup of the water in a small bowl and stir to dissolve. Set aside 15 minutes.

2. In a large bowl, combine 4½ cups unbleached flour, whole wheat flour, salt, and the coarse cornmeal. Add the remaining warm water and mix well. Dough will be sticky. Add additional unbleached flour as necessary to make a dough firm enough to knead. Turn out onto a lightly floured board and knead until dough is shiny, elastic, and smooth, about 15 minutes.

3. Put dough in a lightly oiled bowl and turn to coat with oil. Cover and let rise until doubled in bulk, about 1½ hours. Punch down and let rise, covered, an additional hour.

4. Render pancetta in a skillet over moderate heat until crisp. Drain, cool, and crumble coarsely. Punch dough down and knead in pancetta and mozzarella. Form into 1 large round or 2 smaller loaves. Place on a baking sheet dusted with fine cornmeal. Cover and let rise until doubled in bulk, about 1 hour.

5. Preheat oven to 425° F. Brush tops of loaves with water. Let dry 5 minutes, then brush again. Bake 10 minutes at 425° F, then reduce heat to 350° F. Bake until bread is golden brown and sounds hollow when tapped, an additional 25 to 30 minutes. Cool on racks before slicing.

Makes 1 large or 2 small loaves.

PANE DI MATTINA ALLA SICILIANA
Sicilian morning bread

Sicily's alternative to the morning Danish is a subtly sweet egg bread fragrant with lemon, Marsala, and fennel. The dough has a long, slow rising to ensure its good flavor and texture; to have it for breakfast, make it a day ahead and rewarm it the following morning.

    1 teaspoon olive oil
    1 package active dry yeast
    ½ cup plus 1 teaspoon sugar
    1⅓ cups scalded milk, cooled
       to 100° F
    6½ cups (approximately)
       unbleached flour
    ¼ cup dried currants
    ⅓ cup golden raisins
    ⅓ cup Marsala
    ½ cup unsalted butter
    3 tablespoons shortening
    1½ teaspoons fennel seed
    4 eggs
    1 tablespoon grated lemon rind
    ½ teaspoon salt

Egg Wash

    1 tablespoon whipping cream
    1 egg yolk
    ½ tablespoon Marsala

1. Brush olive oil over surface of a large stainless steel bowl. Put yeast and 1 teaspoon of the sugar in bottom of bowl. Add 1 cup of the scalded milk and stir to dissolve yeast. Set aside for 10 minutes, then add 1½ cups of the flour and the remaining milk. Knead by hand or with a mixer and dough hook until dough is soft and silky, about 7 or 8 minutes. Cover and let rise 5 hours.

2. While dough rises, soak currants and raisins in Marsala for at least 1 hour. In a small saucepan over low heat, melt butter and 2 tablespoons of the shortening. Add fennel seed, remove from heat, and let stand until cool. Add eggs to fennel-seed mixture one at a time, blending well after each addition, then add lemon rind and the remaining sugar. Set aside.

3. When dough has risen 5 hours, add fennel-seed mixture and mix well. Add salt and begin adding the remaining flour, ½ cup at a time. When dough is firm enough to knead, turn out onto a lightly floured board and knead until smooth and soft, about 10 to 15 minutes, adding as much additional flour as necessary to keep it from sticking. During the final 5 minutes, knead in raisins and currants.

4. Form dough into 2 loaves. Use remaining shortening to grease two 9-inch loaf pans. Place dough in pans, cover and let rise until doubled in bulk. This may take as long as 3 hours. (Dough may also be formed into 1 large round loaf and baked free-form.)

5. Preheat oven to 375° F. Brush Egg Wash on loaves 5 minutes before baking. Brush again immediately before baking. Bake until loaves are golden brown and sound hollow when tapped, about 35 minutes. Cool on racks.

Makes two 9-inch loaves or one large round loaf.

Egg Wash Combine cream, yolk, and Marsala in a small bowl.

PANE GIALLO
Polenta bread

This cornbread from northern Italy bears a strong resemblance to American spoon bread: It's lightened with egg whites and baked to an almost pudding-like texture. Red peppers and garlic mark it as distinctly Italian, however, and it is served in the same contexts as its cousin, polenta: with grilled chicken or chops, roast quail, or pan-fried sausages.

  5 tablespoons unsalted butter
  2 tablespoons minced garlic
  1 cup polenta (coarse yellow
      cornmeal)
1½ teaspoons salt
  1 teaspoon freshly ground black
      pepper
  3 eggs, separated
  2 cups milk
  ½ cup half-and-half
  1 cup Roasted Red Peppers
      (see page 14), minced
      Olive oil

1. In a small skillet over moderately low heat, melt 2 tablespoons of the butter. Add garlic and sauté until fragrant. Remove from heat. Combine polenta, salt, and pepper in a bowl and set aside.

2. Put egg yolks, milk, and half-and-half in a saucepan and whisk well. Bring to a boil, whisking constantly. Add cornmeal mixture gradually, then add garlic and red peppers. Cook 2 minutes, stirring constantly with a wooden spoon. Add the remaining butter and cook an additional 2 minutes.

3. Preheat oven to 375° F. Brush an 8-cup soufflé dish or casserole with olive oil. Place dish in oven 5 minutes to warm it. Beat egg whites with a pinch of salt until stiff peaks form. Gently fold whites into thickened cornmeal. Pour mixture into hot soufflé dish. Bake until puffed and golden, about 30 minutes. Serve immediately.

Serves 8.

A richly scented call to rise and shine, Pane di Mattina alla Siciliana is flavored with lemon, Marsala, and fennel. With caffè latte (see page 118), it's a very Italian way to start the day.

The flat bread called focaccia is a popular children's snack but it can also accompany a meal. Serve this onion-and-herb version with soup or salad for a casual lunch.

FOCACCIA
Italian flatbread

By most accounts, *focaccia* is reckoned to be Italy's oldest bread—a simple yeast dough flattened and baked on a stone slab in a wood-fired hearth. Quite likely, it's the grandfather of the famous Neapolitan pizza. Today's cooks can easily make this versatile country bread at home, even without the stone and the hearth. Garnished as you like—here, with sautéed onions and basil—it can partner salads and soups, sliced tomatoes and cheese, or cocktails.

1¼ cups warm (105° F) water
¾ teaspoon sugar
1 package active dry yeast
2¾ cups unbleached flour
3 tablespoons unsalted butter
½ cup minced onion
⅓ cup minced fresh basil
1½ teaspoons coarse salt
½ teaspoon freshly ground black pepper
2 tablespoons olive oil plus olive oil for drizzling
Cornmeal, for dusting

1. Combine ½ cup of the water, the sugar, and yeast in a large bowl. Set aside 10 minutes. Stir in ¾ cup of the flour, cover, and let rise 2½ hours.

2. While dough is rising, heat butter in a skillet over low heat. Add onion and sauté until onion is soft but not browned, about 15 minutes. Remove from heat and stir in basil, ½ teaspoon of the salt, and pepper.

3. Add the remaining flour to dough and beat well. Combine the 2 tablespoons olive oil and remaining warm water, then add to dough. Beat until dough forms a mass. Turn out onto a lightly floured surface and knead until dough is shiny and smooth, 8 to 10 minutes. Transfer dough to a lightly oiled bowl and turn to coat all sides with oil. Cover and let rise until doubled in bulk, about 1½ hours.

4. Preheat oven to 450° F. Punch dough down and roll into a 13- by 15-inch rectangle. Transfer to a baking sheet sprinkled with cornmeal. Spread top with onion mixture. Drizzle with additional olive oil. Sprinkle with the remaining coarse salt and bake until golden, about 15 minutes. Cool slightly on a rack; serve warm.

Makes one 13- by 15-inch rectangle.

FOCACCIA DI PALERMO
Stuffed focaccia with sausage

The Sicilian cooks of Palermo have their own version of *focaccia*: a stuffed rendition that's rather like a sandwich. Any pizza topping will work. Here, a stuffing of garlicky sausage and cheese makes this a hearty luncheon dish.

- 1 recipe Focaccia (opposite page); see instructions below
- ½ pound sweet Italian sausage, casings removed, cooked, and crumbled
- ½ cup ricotta
- ¼ cup freshly grated Parmesan
- ⅓ cup minced Italian parsley
- 3 tablespoons minced onion
- 1 teaspoon minced garlic
  Salt
  Cornmeal, for dusting
- ¼ cup grated mozzarella, provolone, or jack cheese
  Olive oil

1. Prepare step 1 of Focaccia recipe.

2. While dough is rising, combine sausage, ricotta, Parmesan, parsley, onion, and garlic. Taste; add salt if desired. Refrigerate while dough rises.

3. Complete step 3 of recipe for Focaccia.

4. When dough has doubled in bulk, divide it in half. Roll into 2 rectangles of equal size.

5. Preheat oven to 450° F. Dust a baking sheet with cornmeal and transfer one of the rectangles to the baking sheet. Spread filling over the top, leaving a ½-inch border. Sprinkle with grated cheese. Top with second rectangle and crimp the edges. Brush top with olive oil and sprinkle with salt. Bake until golden, about 15 to 20 minutes. Transfer to a rack to cool 10 minutes, then serve.

Serves 4.

PIZZA

Probably no Italian dish is as familiar to Americans as pizza. In fact we tend to think of it as our own invention, although it almost certainly originated in Naples. The basic dough, rolled thin, can be topped with whatever is best and freshest. In Naples that usually means fresh mozzarella and vine-ripened tomatoes. In your house it can mean the best from your garden (see page 54) or a freshly made Pesto Genovese (see page 55). For a delicious switch, fold the pizza in half before baking to make a Calzone (see page 55).

BASIC PIZZA DOUGH

A little rye flour adds distinctive flavor to this basic dough. The recipe can be doubled. For toppings, see the recipes that follow.

- ½ cup warm (105° F) water
- ½ teaspoon sugar
- ½ package active dry yeast
- 2 cups plus 2 tablespoons unbleached white flour
- 2 tablespoons rye flour
- ½ teaspoon salt
- 1 tablespoon olive oil
  Cornmeal, for dusting

1. Combine the water and sugar in a small bowl; sprinkle yeast over it, stir to dissolve, then set aside 10 minutes.

2. Set aside ½ cup unbleached flour. Combine the remaining unbleached flour with rye flour and salt in a large bowl. Stir in yeast mixture and olive oil. Put reserved ½ cup flour on a flat work surface. Turn out dough onto floured surface and knead, slowly incorporating the additional flour. Knead until smooth, about 10 minutes. Transfer dough to a bowl brushed with olive oil; turn dough to coat all sides with oil. Cover and let rise 30 minutes.

3. Punch dough down and divide in half. Roll each half into an 8-inch round; transfer rounds to a baking sheet dusted with cornmeal. Dough is now ready to be topped and baked.

Makes enough dough for two 8-inch pizzas.

PIZZA DEL NORTE
Fontina and provolone pizza alla Valle d'Aosta

The mountainous northern region of Italy known as the Valle d'Aosta is the source of one of the country's finest cheeses: fontina. An excellent melting cheese with a buttery, nutty flavor, it is used in *fonduta*, the Italian version of fondue; here, it transforms a tomato-and-cheese pizza into a memorable dish.

- 1 recipe Basic Pizza Dough (at left)
  Olive oil
- 1½ cups peeled, seeded, and chopped fresh tomato (see page 29)
- 6 ounces Italian fontina, in thin slices
- 3 tablespoons paper-thin garlic slices
- ¼ cup diced provolone
- ¼ cup coarsely chopped parsley, preferably Italian parsley
- 4 ounces Parmesan
  Additional minced parsley, for garnish (optional)

Preheat oven to 425° F. Roll dough out into two rounds according to instructions in Basic Pizza Dough and transfer to baking sheet. Brush surface with olive oil. Divide tomatoes among the two rounds. Top with fontina, garlic, provolone, and parsley. Use a cheese slicer to shave thin sheets of Parmesan over tops of pizzas. Drizzle with olive oil. Bake until the edges are browned and the top is bubbly, about 12 to 15 minutes. Garnish with additional parsley, if desired.

Makes two 8-inch pizzas.

What's a calzone? In short, a folded-over pizza. This one reveals its filling of spinach, prosciutto, and molten cheeses.

PIZZA DELL' ESTATE
Summer garden pizza

This simple pizza from Palermo is a fine way to show off your garden tomatoes. Non-gardeners should buy the best vine-ripened tomatoes available. A fruity olive oil and the best-quality whole-milk mozzarella are other musts.

> 1 large, ripe tomato, peeled, seeded, and chopped
>
> 3 tablespoons minced fresh basil
>
> 4 tablespoons olive oil
>
> 2 tablespoons minced shallot or green onion
>
> 1 recipe Basic Pizza Dough (see page 53)
>
> 3 tablespoons minced garlic
>
> ½ cup paper-thin red onion slices
>
> 6 ounces whole-milk mozzarella, grated
>
> 6 tablespoons freshly grated Parmesan
>
> 2 anchovy fillets, julienned (optional)
>
> Additional olive oil

1. Combine tomato, basil, 2 tablespoons of the olive oil, and shallots; set aside to marinate for at least 30 minutes or up to 8 hours. Combine garlic and the remaining olive oil in a small bowl and set aside for 30 minutes.

2. Preheat oven to 425° F. Roll dough out according to instructions in Basic Pizza Dough and transfer to baking sheet. Combine garlic and tomato mixtures and divide between the two rounds. Top with onion slices, mozzarella, and Parmesan. Arrange anchovies (if used) on top. Drizzle surface with a little additional olive oil. Bake until the edges are browned and the top is bubbly, about 12 to 15 minutes. Serve immediately.

Makes two 8-inch pizzas.

CALZONE
Stuffed pizza turnover

A calzone is a pizza by another name: Mound the filling on half the dough and fold the other half over to form the bulging half-moon shape of this clever creation from Venice. Small ones are eaten out of hand, as a snack or a quick lunch; large ones are served with a knife and fork. Cutting into a hot calzone and releasing the molten filling is part of the pleasure of this fragrant dish, but small ones should be cooled slightly to firm the filling and avoid burning fingers.

> 1½ cups cooked fresh spinach, squeezed dry
> 1¼ cups ricotta
> 3 tablespoons freshly grated Parmesan
> ¼ cup pitted and chopped Greek Calamata olives
> ¼ cup minced parsley
> 1 recipe Basic Pizza Dough (see page 53)
> ½ cup shredded prosciutto
> ½ cup grated whole-milk mozzarella
> 1 egg mixed with 1 tablespoon water
> Olive oil

Preheat oven to 475° F. Combine spinach, ricotta, Parmesan, olives, and parsley. Roll dough out on a lightly floured surface into 1 large or 2 small rounds, ¼ inch thick. Place spinach mixture on bottom half of the dough, leaving a ⅝-inch border. Top spinach with prosciutto and mozzarella. Brush border with egg mixture, then fold top half over the bottom and seal the edges. Brush top with olive oil. Bake until golden, about 12 to 15 minutes. Brush again with olive oil. If calzone will be eaten out of hand, let cool slightly before serving.

Makes two 4-inch or one 8-inch calzone.

---

menu

A PIZZA PARTY

*Bagna Cauda
(see page 19)*

Pizza al Pesto

Pizza alle Vongole

Pizza Rossa

Amaretti Sundaes

Wine and Coffee

What better way to ring in the New Year or fete that monumental fortieth birthday than with a lighthearted pizza party for adults only? Begin with cocktails or white wine and a grand Bagna Cauda, then bring on the Chianti Classico and the pizzas. For dessert, set out vanilla ice cream, crushed amaretti cookies, whipped cream, and hot fudge sauce, and let guests invent their own little bit of heaven.

NEAPOLITAN PIZZA DOUGH

The classic Neapolitan pizza dough has no oil in it. It yields a drier crust that can support a moist topping.

> 2 tablespoons dry yeast
> 1 cup warm (105° F) water
> 4½ cups (approximately) flour
> 1 teaspoon salt

Dissolve yeast in the water in a medium bowl. Add 2 cups of the flour, mix well to make a sponge, cover, and let rise 45 minutes. In a large bowl, combine 2 cups of the remaining flour and the salt. Add risen sponge and mix well. Turn out onto a lightly floured surface and knead until smooth and silky, about 5 minutes, adding flour as necessary. Put dough in a lightly oiled bowl, turn to coat all sides with oil, cover and let rise 2 hours. Punch down dough and divide in halves, quarters, or eighths, depending on desired pizza size. Roll and top as desired.

Makes enough dough for 8 small, 4 medium, or 2 large pizzas.

PIZZA AL PESTO
Pizza with fresh basil sauce

Despite the simplicity of its ingredients, this pizza is rich and satisfying; don't be tempted to gussy it up with other garnishes. The brilliant green of the pesto is the perfect counterpoint to an all-red Pizza Rossa.

> 1 recipe Neapolitan Pizza Dough (above)
> Cornmeal, for dusting
> 4 ounces mozzarella, sliced
> 1 recipe Pesto Genovese (see page 35)
> ¼ cup pine nuts

Preheat oven to 475° F. Divide dough into 2, 4, or 8 portions, as desired. Roll out on a lightly floured surface into rounds ⅓ inch thick. Transfer to a baking sheet dusted with cornmeal. Arrange mozzarella over dough; brush each round with a thin layer of pesto. Garnish with pine nuts and bake until browned and bubbly, 12 to 18 minutes depending on size.

Makes 8 small, 4 medium, or 2 large pizzas.

Begin a Pizza Party with a basket of colorful vegetables and an anchovy-garlic dip; follow with three rustic, crusty pizzas. Recipes begin on page 55.

PIZZA ALLE VONGOLE
Pizza with fresh clams

Rubbery, canned clams and over-cooked tomato sauce are the norm on restaurant clam pizzas. You can make a far better version at home with fresh, chopped tomatoes and freshly steamed clams. To keep the clams from toughening, add them just as the pizza comes out of the oven.

2½ cups seeded and chopped tomatoes (see page 29)
⅓ cup plus 2 tablespoons olive oil
2 tablespoons minced fresh oregano
1 recipe Neapolitan Pizza Dough (see page 55)
Cornmeal, for dusting
2 tablespoons minced garlic
1 cup dry white wine
3½ pounds small clams
2 tablespoons coarsely chopped Italian parsley

1. Preheat oven to 475° F. In a small bowl, combine tomatoes, ⅓ cup of the olive oil, and the oregano; let stand 15 minutes.

2. Divide dough into 2, 4, or 8 portions, as desired. Roll out dough on a lightly floured surface into rounds ⅓ inch thick. Transfer to a baking sheet dusted with cornmeal. Brush dough rounds with 2 tablespoons of the liquid from the tomatoes. Divide tomatoes among the dough rounds and brush with oil remaining in the tomato bowl. Bake until browned and puffy, 12 to 18 minutes depending on size.

3. While pizza is baking, heat remaining oil over moderately low heat in a kettle or skillet large enough to hold all the clams. Add garlic and sauté until fragrant but not browned, about 2 minutes. Add wine, raise heat to high, and bring to a boil. Add clams, cover, and steam until they open, about 3 to 5 minutes. Shake kettle occasionally and check clams, removing any that have opened. Discard any that haven't opened after 5 minutes.

4. Remove clams from shells; return clams to kettle. Add parsley and remove from heat. Remove pizza from oven when it is done. Scatter clams over the surface. Serve immediately.

Makes 8 small, 4 medium, or 2 large pizzas.

PIZZA ROSSA
All-red pizza

Sun-dried tomatoes have a sweet intensity that's almost candylike. Just a few, cut in strips, will enrich and enliven fresh tomatoes. Add some sweet height-of-summer red peppers and you have a brassy, bright-red topping for a warm-weather pizza.

3 tablespoons olive oil
3 tablespoons minced garlic
2½ cups seeded and chopped tomatoes (see page 29)
¼ cup chopped fresh basil
1 recipe Neapolitan Pizza Dough (see page 55)
Cornmeal, for dusting baking sheet
Additional olive oil
1 recipe Roasted Red Peppers (see page 14)
¼ cup julienned sun-dried tomatoes (from jar)
2 tablespoons oil from sun-dried tomatoes
¼ cup coarsely grated Parmesan

1. Heat olive oil over moderately low heat in a large skillet. Add garlic and sauté gently until fragrant but not browned, about 3 minutes. Add fresh tomatoes and basil; stir to mix and remove from heat.

2. Preheat oven to 475° F. Divide pizza dough in 2, 4, or 8 portions, as desired. Roll out dough on a lightly floured surface into rounds ⅓ inch thick. Transfer to a baking sheet dusted with cornmeal. Brush rounds lightly with olive oil. Divide fresh tomato mixture among rounds. Top with Roasted Red Peppers; garnish with sun-dried tomato. Drizzle with tomato oil and dust with Parmesan. Bake until browned and bubbly, 12 to 18 minutes depending on size.

Makes 8 small, 4 medium, or 2 large pizzas.

GRAINS

Because grains are inexpensive, nutritious, and easily stored, they've long dominated the cooking of Italian peasants. Today these frugal cooks' creations are favorites among even the well-heeled, although admittedly the dishes have been refined from their humble beginnings. Polenta is now on restaurant menus all over the north, served with game birds or with melted fontina cheese and shaved truffles. Hardly humble!

The famous Arborio rice from the Po Valley can also be served plain or fancy. At its simplest it's cooked with stock to make a modest risotto (see page 61), but when the pocketbook allows, it's dressed up with shrimp, saffron, or wild mushrooms.

Italy's grain-based dishes change with the whim of the cook and the season. The following recipes are only a glimpse of the possibilities.

BASIC POLENTA
Cornmeal mush

Polenta must be watched and stirred continuously as it cooks, but diligence yields delicious results: a thick, creamy, golden pudding that has inspired cooks to countless variations. Common throughout northern Italy, polenta can be eaten hot, or it can be poured into a pan, cooled until firm, and sliced. In that form it can be layered with meat sauces, or mushrooms and cheese, and baked until bubbly. Serve the following recipe hot from the pan, to partner grilled sausages, chicken, or chops.

4 cups water
1½ teaspoons coarse salt
1 cup polenta (see page 9)
4 tablespoons unsalted butter
¼ cup freshly grated Parmesan

In a heavy saucepan bring water and salt to a boil. Gradually add polenta, whisking constantly. Stir in half of the butter. Cook over low heat, stirring continuously with a wood spoon, for 20 minutes. Mixture will become quite thick. Stir in remaining butter and Parmesan and serve immediately.

Serves 4.

POLENTA CON GORGONZOLA
Polenta with Gorgonzola

With a simple green salad, this delectable Venetian dish is a meal in itself. Use only best-quality imported Gorgonzola.

　1　recipe Basic Polenta
　　　(opposite page)
　6　ounces Gorgonzola, crumbled
　¼　cup whipping cream

1. Preheat oven to 350° F. Prepare polenta. Stir half the Gorgonzola into hot polenta. Pour it into an 11- by 13-inch baking dish. Cool slightly to firm the polenta.

2. Pour cream over the top and dot with the remaining cheese. Bake about 15 minutes, until cream is absorbed and cheese melts.

Serves 4.

POLENTA ALLA GRIGLIA
Grilled polenta

When cooled until firm, then sliced and grilled, polenta makes a great companion to "saucy" dishes. Serve it with braised rabbit or veal stew, with Ragù Bolognese (see page 36), or with fat sausages sautéed with peppers.

　1　recipe Basic Polenta
　　　(opposite page)

1. Oil an 8- or 9-inch loaf pan or a 1-inch-deep cake pan. Pour hot polenta into prepared pan. Cool, then chill until firm.

2. Prepare a medium-hot charcoal fire. Oil the grilling rack. Slice polenta ½ inch thick. Grill on both sides until hot throughout. The polenta may also be successfully cooked on an indoor griddle. Serve immediately.

Serves 4.

There are probably as many ways to cook polenta as there are cooks. Here, a creamy version both mixed and topped with Gorgonzola contrasts with Polenta alla Griglia, which has been cooled till firm, then grilled.

The classic Risotto alla Milanese is made with saffron and the short, plump Italian Arborio rice. Shown here is a Roman version flavored with lemon juice and rind. It makes a good first course before Gamberi con Peperoni e Prosciutto (see page 69), grilled salmon or tuna, or a brochette of swordfish and artichokes.

RISO CON GAMBERI
Rice with Venetian shrimp

Whether this dish can be called authentic without the splendid Venetian scampi is a question for nitpickers only. Americans can make it with medium shrimp, what the Italians call *gamberi*, and it will still be an exquisite first course.

> 1   tablespoon olive oil
> 2   tablespoons butter
> 2   tablespoons minced shallot
> 1   cup raw Arborio rice
> 2   cups fish stock
> ¼   cup tomato purée
> 16 to 18 medium shrimp (about
>   1¼ lb), shelled and deveined
>   Salt and freshly ground black
>   pepper
> 2   tablespoons minced parsley

1. Heat olive oil and butter in a saucepan over moderately low heat. Add shallot and sauté gently until softened, about 5 minutes. Add rice and cook, stirring, for 1 minute. Add fish stock and tomato purée. Bring to a boil. Cover, reduce heat to low, and cook 8 minutes.

2. Arrange shrimp on top of rice, recover, and cook until shrimp are just done, about 7 minutes more. Add salt and pepper to taste. Pour rice into a warm serving platter and arrange shrimp on top. Dust with parsley and serve immediately in warm bowls.

Serves 4.

RISI E BISI
Italian rice with fresh peas

The first spring peas prompt Venetian cooks to make Risi e Bisi. It is a popular first course, usually thin enough to require a bowl and spoon.

    1   tablespoon olive oil
    4   tablespoons unsalted butter
    3   tablespoons minced shallot
    1   cup Arborio rice, uncooked
    3   cups chicken stock
    ¾   pound shelled fresh peas
    6   tablespoons freshly grated
        Parmesan
    3   tablespoons minced fresh basil
    1   tablespoon minced parsley
        Coarse salt

Heat olive oil and 3 tablespoons of the butter in a saucepan over moderately low heat. Add shallots; sauté gently until softened, about 5 minutes. Add rice; cook, stirring, for 1 minute. Add stock, bring to a boil, cover, and reduce heat to low. Cook 2 minutes. Add peas and remaining butter. Cook until rice and peas are just tender, 8 to 10 minutes more. Stir in Parmesan, basil, and parsley. Salt to taste. Serve immediately.

Serves 4.

RISOTTO AL LIMONE
Lemon risotto

Serve this sprightly Roman risotto before a fish main course.

    2   tablespoons plus 2 teaspoons
        unsalted butter
    2   tablespoons olive oil
    ¼   cup minced onion
        Grated rind of 1 lemon
    1½ cups Arborio rice, uncooked
    4½ cups hot chicken stock
    ¼   cup plus 2 teaspoons
        lemon juice
    ½   cup freshly grated Parmesan

1. In a heavy saucepan over moderately low heat, melt 2 tablespoons of the butter and the olive oil. Add onion and lemon rind; sauté slowly for 5 minutes. Add rice; stir to coat with oil. Turn up heat to high; toast rice, stirring, for 30 seconds. Immediately add ½ cup of the stock; reduce

heat to medium-low and stir until stock is absorbed. Add more, ½ cup at a time, stirring constantly and adding more only when previous portion has been absorbed. When all stock is absorbed (about 20 to 25 minutes), stir in ¼ cup of the lemon juice. The rice should be tender. If not, add warm water bit by bit until rice is tender yet firm.

2. Stir in Parmesan and remaining butter. Cook briefly to blend and melt cheese. Season to taste with salt and pepper. Add remaining lemon juice; serve immediately in warm bowls.

Serves 4.

Risotto alla Milanese Omit lemon rind and lemon juice. Increase chicken stock to 4¾ cups. Add ¼ teaspoon saffron threads or ⅛ teaspoon powdered saffron to hot chicken stock.

RISO DELL' AUTUNNO
Italian rice with autumn vegetables

A trio of late-harvest vegetables—eggplant, celery, and mushrooms—added to a traditional Milanese risotto yields a filling dish for a simple autumn dinner.

    1   recipe Risotto al Limone
        (at left)
    ½   cup olive oil
    2   tablespoons unsalted butter
    ¼   cup minced onion
    2   tablespoons minced garlic
    1   large eggplant (about 1 to
        1¼ lb), peeled and cut into
        ½-inch dice
    ½   teaspoon hot red-pepper flakes
    ½   cup minced celery
    1   cup cooked garbanzo or
        kidney beans (rinsed and
        drained, if canned)
    ½   cup quartered mushrooms
    1   teaspoon minced fresh
        rosemary (optional)
    ¼   cup minced parsley
        Salt and freshly ground black
        pepper
    2   tablespoons freshly grated
        Parmesan

1. Make Risotto al Limone and set aside. Heat oil and butter in a large

skillet over moderate heat. Add onion and garlic and sauté until fragrant and slightly softened, about 3 minutes. Add eggplant and brown on all sides. Add hot-pepper flakes and celery and cook an additional 3 minutes. Remove from heat.

2. Preheat oven to 375° F. Stir beans, mushrooms, rosemary (if used), and half of the parsley into eggplant mixture. Combine vegetables and risotto. Season to taste with salt and pepper. Transfer to a buttered 2-quart casserole, cover, and bake until heated through, about 20 minutes. Serve from casserole, topped with remaining parsley and Parmesan.

Serves 4.

GNOCCHI ALLA ROMANA
Baked semolina gnocchi

Cooked semolina enriched with butter, cheese, and eggs is the basis for the classic Roman *gnocchi*.

    ½   cup butter
    2   egg yolks
    1   tablespoon kosher salt
    1   cup grated Parmesan
    4¼ cups milk
    1   cup plus 1 tablespoon
        semolina

1. Combine 3 tablespoons of the butter, the egg yolks and salt, and ¾ cup of the Parmesan. Set aside.

2. Put milk in large saucepan and bring to a simmer over medium heat. Pour in semolina in a steady stream, whisking constantly. Cook, stirring occasionally, until thickened and smooth. Remove from heat; immediately stir in cheese mixture. Pour onto an oiled baking sheet, spread ¼ inch thick, and cool ½ hour.

3. Preheat oven to 400° F. Cut cooled mixture into diamonds or rounds. Spread 2 tablespoons of the butter in an ovenproof 8-inch dish. Place gnocchi in dish in a single layer, slightly overlapping. Dot remaining butter over top; sprinkle with remaining Parmesan. Bake 10 minutes. Place under broiler until crust forms (1 to 2 minutes). Serve piping hot.

Makes about 20, serves 4 to 5.

Surrounded by water, Italy boasts a wealth of seafood. From scampi to swordfish to salt cod, fish and shellfish are fundamental to Italian cuisine.

Fish & Shellfish

Increasingly, Americans are cooking and eating fish and shellfish; Italians always have. In this chapter you'll find recipes for preparing seafood in a wide variety of ways, from grilling (see Gamberi del Veneto, page 70) and frying (see Frutte di Mare Fritti, page 66) to braising (see Calamari Verdi, page 65) and roasting (see Cozze al Forno, page 66). Step-by-step photographs show how to clean squid (see page 66) and open clams, oysters, and mussels (page 67). A highlight of the chapter is a menu for a Lakeside Picnic (see page 70).

Offer bibs and finger bowls when you serve Brodetto alla Napoletana, the spicy southern Italian version of shellfish stew.

FISH AND SHELLFISH

As you might expect in a country bordered by water on three sides, fish and shellfish figure prominently in the Italian diet. From tiny anchovies to giant Sicilian swordfish, there are few sea creatures that Italians don't eat. Neapolitan clams, Sardinian tuna, Genoese eels, and Venetian scampi have reputations that extend far beyond their regions.

The Adriatic yields red mullet and sole, sardines and squid, spiny lobster and shrimp of all sizes. From the lakes of Lombardy and the mountain streams of Piedmont come trout, carp, and fresh-water eels. Some observers find it ironic that a country so rich in fresh fish should have developed an abiding passion for salt cod. But once you taste Baccalà Fritto alla Siciliana (see page 44) or Baccalà del Venerdì (see page 69), you'll understand what good cooking can do to a "poor man's fish."

The good cooking extends to recipes such as Brodetto alla Napoletana (opposite page), Calamari Fritti (see page 66), and Gamberi del Veneto (see page 70), to name only a few of the seafood dishes that form an integral part of Italian fare.

OSTRICHE TREVISIANE
Grilled oysters Treviso style

A warm, grilled-oyster salad makes an unusual first course, served with sparkling wine or an Italian Verdicchio. The smoky juices from the oysters are whisked into the vinaigrette just before it's drizzled over the salad. For best results, choose sturdy, colorful lettuces with a slightly bitter edge, like curly endive and red radicchio.

        2 tablespoons lemon juice
        ½ cup olive oil
        1 teaspoon grated lemon rind
        2 tablespoons minced parsley
        2 tablespoons minced
            green onion
        ½ teaspoon salt
        ½ teaspoon freshly ground
            black pepper
        1 small head curly endive
        1 small head radicchio
       30 fresh oysters
            Freshly ground black pepper

1. Prepare a medium-hot charcoal fire in grill.

2. To make dressing: Combine lemon juice, olive oil, lemon rind, parsley, green onion, salt, and pepper. Whisk well and set aside.

3. Separate lettuces into individual leaves; wash well and dry thoroughly. Tear large leaves into small pieces. Arrange on a serving platter.

4. When charcoal fire is ready, position rack above the coals and set oysters directly on the rack. After about 2½ minutes, they will begin to open. They should be fully open and hot after about 3½ minutes. Be careful not to overcook. Discard any that don't open.

5. Remove oysters as they open. Pour oyster liquor into a small bowl. Remove oysters from shells and arrange them atop the lettuce. Add reserved oyster liquor to dressing and whisk well. Taste and adjust salt if necessary; pour dressing over oysters. Grind some black pepper over the top and serve immediately.

Serves 6 as an appetizer.

BRODETTO ALLA NAPOLETANA
Neapolitan shellfish stew

Shellfish soup as made in Naples is usually loaded with mussels and clams, invariably spiked with hot peppers, and often served atop toasted bread. It's a gutsy soup to eat with gusto, accompanied by a rough white wine. You can add saffron, prawns, and crab to dress it up a bit for company, but it's still a dish for guests who don't mind getting their fingers messy. Bibs and finger bowls are a good idea.

- 12 small, fresh clams
- 1 quart water
- 2 tablespoons cornmeal
- 12 fresh mussels
- 1 cup dry white wine
- 1 onion, coarsely chopped
- 3 cloves garlic, peeled and smashed (not minced)
- ½ teaspoon hot red-pepper flakes
- 1 tablespoon butter
- 3 tablespoons olive oil
- ½ cup minced carrot
- ½ cup minced celery
- ½ cup minced red or yellow bell pepper
- ½ pound white potatoes, peeled and cut into ½-inch cubes
- 2 cups peeled, seeded, and chopped tomatoes (see page 29)
- ¾ teaspoon saffron threads dissolved in 2 tablespoons hot fish stock
- 3½ cups fish stock, preferably homemade, or bottled clam juice
- 8 jumbo shrimp or prawns in shells
- ½ pound shelled crabmeat or 1 cooked Dungeness crab, broken into manageable sections and cracked
  Coarse salt
- ½ cup minced green onion
- 3 tablespoons minced parsley
  Bruschetta (see page 13)

1. Scrub clams and put them in a bowl with water and cornmeal. Soak 2 hours to rid clams of any grit. Drain and set aside. Scrub mussels and remove beards (see page 67). Set aside.

2. Combine wine, onion, garlic, and red-pepper flakes in a large, lidded pot and bring to a boil over high heat. Add clams and mussels and cover. Reduce heat to medium and steam covered, 3 to 7 minutes. After 3 minutes, begin checking clams and mussels, removing any that have opened. Discard any that haven't opened after 7 minutes.

3. Heat butter and oil in a large pot over moderate heat. Add carrot, celery, bell pepper, and potatoes. Sauté vegetables gently for 7 minutes. Add tomatoes and cook another 5 minutes. Remove clams and mussels from broth and set aside. Strain the broth through a double thickness of cheesecloth and reserve. Add saffron, stock, and reserved steaming liquid and simmer 10 minutes. The vegetables should be thoroughly tender. Add prawns, cover, and simmer until prawns turn bright pink. Add crab and heat about 30 seconds. Add clams and mussels and heat through gently. Taste and add salt if necessary. Stir in green onions and remove from heat.

4. Ladle soup into warmed tureen or into warmed soup bowls. Garnish with parsley and serve with a basket of Bruschetta. Pass the pepper mill at the table.

Serves 4 to 5.

CALAMARI VERDI
Braised spinach-stuffed squid

Whole squid lend themselves perfectly to savory stuffings of all kinds. Here, in a Florentine dish, they're plumped with spinach, basil, and rice, then braised with garlic, more spinach, and wine. The result is tender squid in a delicious green sauce, to serve as is or on a bed of lemony rice.

- 4 pounds fresh squid
- ½ cup cooked rice, preferably short-grain Arborio
- 8 cups chopped fresh spinach leaves
- ¼ cup chopped fresh basil
- ½ cup minced onion
- ½ tablespoon minced garlic
- ¼ cup olive oil
- ½ cup white wine
- 2 teaspoons white wine vinegar
- 2 teaspoons tomato paste
- 1 teaspoon coarse salt
  Lemon wedges, for garnish
- 3 tablespoons minced parsley, for garnish

1. Clean squid, removing tentacles (see page 66). Chop tentacles coarsely; leave bodies whole. In a bowl, combine chopped tentacles, rice, 4 cups of the spinach, 1 tablespoon of the basil, 1 tablespoon of the onion, and a pinch of the garlic. Moisten with a little of the olive oil and 1 tablespoon of the wine.

2. In a large saucepan or stockpot, heat 1 tablespoon olive oil over high heat; add rice-spinach mixture. Sauté, stirring constantly, until spinach just wilts. Remove from heat and let cool. Stuff squid bodies loosely with cooled mixture, saving any extra stuffing for the sauce.

3. In a Dutch oven, heat remaining olive oil over moderate heat. Add remaining onion and garlic; sauté until softened. Add stuffed squid bodies; sauté about 12 minutes. They should color slightly. Add remaining wine and the vinegar; cook gently until wine evaporates. Add tomato paste and remaining spinach, remaining basil, the salt, and any leftover stuffing. Cover; cook slowly for 15 to 20 minutes. Squid should be quite tender; most of liquid in pan will have evaporated. Transfer to a serving platter and surround with lemon wedges. Garnish with parsley.

Serves 4.

CLEANING SQUID

1. *Rinse squid in cold water. Cut off tentacles just above eye. Squeeze thick center part of tentacles, pushing out the hard beak. Discard beak.*

2. *Squeeze the entrails from the body by running fingers from the closed to the cut end. Pull out the transparent quill that protrudes from body.*

3. *Slip a finger under the skin; peel it off. Pull off edible fins and skin them.*

COZZE AL FORNO
Roasted mussels

Roasting mussels in the dry heat of an oven *(il forno)* seems to intensify their flavor. Simple Italian pizza restaurants often offer mussels this way, baking them in the searing-hot, wood-fired oven and serving them in the baking dish so that diners can mop up the fragrant juices with bread. To approximate this Genoese dish at home, preheat your oven to its highest setting 30 minutes ahead.

> 2 tablespoons minced fresh basil
> ½ tablespoon minced fresh oregano
> 2 teaspoons minced garlic
> 1 teaspoon coarse salt
> ¾ cup olive oil
> 3 dozen fresh mussels
> Freshly ground black pepper
> Lemon wedges

1. Combine basil, oregano, garlic, salt, and oil in a pitcher. Stir to blend and set aside for up to 6 hours.

2. Preheat oven to 500° F. Scrub mussels and remove their beards (see opposite page). Put mussels on a baking sheet in one layer. Bake 4 to 8 minutes. After about 3 minutes, begin checking mussels, removing any open ones to a warmed serving dish. Drizzle the herb-flavored oil over the mussels as you add them to the serving dish. Discard any mussels that have not opened after 8 minutes. When all of the mussels are in the serving dish, grind some black pepper over the top and serve immediately with lemon wedges and any remaining oil.

Serves 4.

CALAMARI FRITTI
Fried squid

For perfect fried squid, choose the smallest you can find, flour them lightly, and monitor the temperature of your oil closely. Fry in small batches to keep the oil at an even 375° F. Fried squid are enjoyed throughout Italy, served hot in a napkin-lined basket with cocktails or a crisp white wine.

> 2 pounds small, fresh squid
> 1½ cups flour
> 1½ teaspoons coarse salt
> 1 teaspoon freshly ground black pepper
> Oil, for deep-frying (1 part olive oil, 3 parts corn oil)
> Lemon wedges

1. Clean squid (at left), remove tentacles, and cut bodies into ¼-inch rings. Combine flour, salt, and pepper in a bag. Dredge squid rings and tentacles in flour, shaking off excess. Transfer floured squid to a plate.

2. Heat about 3 inches of oil in a wok or deep-fryer to 375° F. Use a thermometer to check the oil temperature and to maintain it during frying. Fry squid in batches until golden and crisp, about 1 minute. Transfer with a slotted spoon to a warm baking sheet lined with paper towels. Keep warm in a low oven while you fry the remaining batches. Pile fried squid on a serving platter and surround with lemon wedges.

Serves 4 as an appetizer.

FRUTTE DI MARE FRITTI
Mixed fried shellfish

When freshly shucked, lightly breaded, and quickly fried, these fruits of the sea retain their clean ocean flavors. For easy shucking, invest in a specially designed oyster or clam knife (see opposite page for instructions on opening clams and oysters and cleaning mussels). A cooperative fishmonger will shuck them for you, but you should use them shortly thereafter. Pan-fry them as they do in the southern Italian seaport of Bari and serve with warm anchovy sauce or lemon wedges.

3 slices (approximately 3 oz)
   firm-textured, homemade-type
   white bread, 2 to 3 days old
1 teaspoon coarse salt
¼ teaspoon hot-pepper flakes
½ teaspoon freshly ground
   black pepper
3 eggs
1½ cups flour, for dredging
16 oysters, freshly shucked
   and liquor reserved
16 clams, freshly shucked
16 mussels, freshly shucked
   Bagna Cauda (sauce only;
   see page 19), or lemon wedges
   Olive oil, for frying

1. Grind bread in a food processor or blender to make fine crumbs. You should have about 2½ cups. Stir in salt, pepper flakes, and black pepper. Put in a bowl and set aside.

2. Beat eggs lightly to blend. Put flour in a small bowl. Dredge shellfish lightly in flour, shaking off excess. Dip in eggs, letting excess egg drip off. Dip in bread crumbs and transfer to a plate.

3. If you are using Bagna Cauda, heat it in a small saucepan, add reserved oyster liquor, and keep warm. Have a tray lined with a double thickness of paper towels beside the stove. Set a large skillet over high heat; when it is hot, add just enough olive oil to coat the pan. When oil is almost smoking, add shellfish a few at a time and fry quickly on both sides until golden, adding additional olive oil as necessary. Transfer to paper towels as they are done. To serve, either put a little warm sauce on each of four warm plates and top with shellfish, or garnish shellfish with lemon wedges.

Serves 4.

OPENING BIVALVES

Refrigerate oysters, clams, and mussels, for a few hours or freeze for 30 minutes to relax muscles; they will be easier to open. Then scrub shells thoroughly with a stiff brush under cold water. Soft-shell clams are fragile; take care not to break them.

Oysters

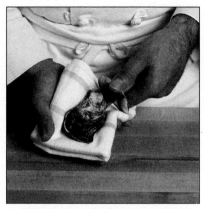

1. *Wearing work gloves or using a heavy cloth, anchor the oyster in the palm of one hand, with the deep cup of the oyster down. Insert tip of oyster knife into hinge and lift up to open shell.*

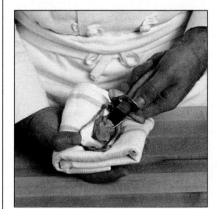

2. *Slide knife along inside of upper shell to sever the muscle that attaches the shell to the flesh. Discard upper shell. Keep oyster level to avoid spilling juices. Slide knife under flesh, being careful not to pierce it, and sever bottom muscle. Remove any bits of broken shell.*

Clams

1. *Slide the blade of a clam knife into the seam between the two shells. Work knife between shells toward the hinge until you can pry the shells apart. Keep clam level to avoid spilling juices, or work over a bowl.*

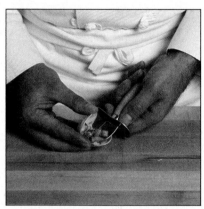

2. *Slide blade along inside of one shell to sever muscles and under clam to dislodge it from shell.*

Mussels

"Debeard" mussel by removing the byssus, the threads of tissue that protrude from the shell. Mussels die soon after debearding, so cook them promptly. Open a mussel as you would a clam.

Swordfish, tomato, and fennel make a tantalizing trio, as in the Sicilian Pesce Spada al Forno con Finocchi. Serve the dish with a crisp white wine.

TONNO DELL' ESTATE
Tuna for the summertime

Grilled tuna, barely cooked, makes a refreshing summer salad when it's dressed with lemon and oil and tossed with tomatoes, peppers, and capers in the style of Genoa. Let it marinate at room temperature for an hour to blend the flavors, or make it a day ahead and refrigerate. Serve the tuna as a first course on a bed of soft lettuce; pass warm bread and a cruet of olive oil. For a stand-up cocktail party, nestle small portions of tuna in tender butter lettuce ''cups'' so guests can eat them taco-style.

> 2 *pounds fresh tuna fillet, in one or two pieces*
> ¼ *cup balsamic vinegar*
> 2 *pounds tomatoes, peeled, seeded, and chopped (see page 29)*
> 1 *cup olive oil*
> ¼ *cup lemon juice*
>   *Pulp of 2 lemons, seeded and cut into ⅓-inch dice*
> ¼ *cup capers*
> 1 *cup minced parsley*
> 1 *cup pitted and chopped Calamata olives*
> 1 *cup diced red bell pepper*
> ½ *cup diced green bell pepper*
> ¼ *cup minced green onion*
> ½ *cup thinly sliced red onion*
>   *Salt and freshly ground black pepper*
>   *Additional olive oil*

1. Prepare a hot charcoal fire. When fire is ready, sear tuna quickly on all sides until outside changes color but inside is still nearly raw. Transfer fish to a baking sheet and pour vinegar over it. When fish is cool, cut it into 1-inch chunks and transfer to a large serving bowl.

2. In a small bowl, combine tomatoes, olive oil, lemon juice, lemon pulp, and capers. Mix well, then add to fish. Add parsley, olives, bell peppers, green onion, and red onion. Stir gently to blend. Let marinate 1 hour at room temperature, or cover and marinate overnight in refrigerator, bringing to room temperature before serving. Season to taste with salt and pepper before serving; add a little more olive oil if salad seems dry.

Serves 4.

GAMBERI CON PEPERONI E PROSCIUTTO
Shrimp with peppers and prosciutto

This Tuscan dish can be made in minutes and served as an appetizer or a main course. The shrimp are steamed with prosciutto and peppers, then glazed with an Italian sweet-and-sour sauce—rich, mellow Marsala balanced by lemon and balsamic vinegar.

- ¼ cup olive oil
- 1 cup diced onion
- 1 tablespoon minced garlic
- ½ cup diced red bell pepper
- ½ cup diced green bell pepper
- ½ cup diced yellow bell pepper
  Pinch hot red-pepper flakes
- 4 ounces prosciutto, thinly sliced
- ¼ cup Marsala
- 16 jumbo shrimp or 24 large shrimp or 32 medium shrimp, shelled
- 1 tablespoon balsamic vinegar
  Salt
- 1 tablespoon minced parsley
- 1 tablespoon minced fresh basil
- 1 teaspoon grated lemon rind

1. Heat olive oil in a large sauté pan over moderate heat. Add onion, garlic, all bell peppers, and pepper flakes. Sauté 3 minutes. Add prosciutto and cook 1 minute longer. Add Marsala and cook 20 seconds.

2. Add shrimp and vinegar, cover, and cook until shrimp turn pink, 4 to 7 minutes, depending on size of shrimp. Be careful not to overcook. Remove shrimp from pan and arrange on a warmed serving platter. Taste the juices in the pan and add salt, if necessary. Spoon peppers and pan juices over shrimp. Combine parsley, basil, and lemon; sprinkle over shrimp. Serve immediately.

Serves 4.

PESCE SPADA AL FORNO CON FINOCCHI
Roasted swordfish with fennel

Sicilian cooks know dozens of ways to prepare their prized swordfish. Here, in a classic dish, it is baked with tomato sauce, fennel, and herbs, bold flavors that might overpower a more delicate fish. Precede it with Spaghetti con Aglio e Olio (see page 37), and follow it with ripe summer peaches in wine (see page 114).

- 3 tablespoons olive oil
- 1 onion, diced
- 1 tablespoon minced garlic
- ¼ cup dry white wine
- ½ cup chopped fresh basil
- ½ cup chopped fresh parsley
- 8 small (2-inch dia) whole bulbs fennel or 4 larger ones cut in half lengthwise (see page 80)
- 2 cups homemade Sugo di Pomodoro (see page 36)
- 2 pounds swordfish steaks
- ¼ cup lemon juice
  Salt and freshly ground black pepper

1. Preheat oven to 400° F. Heat oil in a large sauté pan over moderate heat. Add onion and garlic and sauté until slightly wilted, about 5 minutes. Add wine, basil, parsley, and fennel. Bring to a boil, reduce heat, and simmer, covered, until the fennel begins to soften, about 10 minutes. Transfer mixture to an ovenproof casserole large enough to hold the fish steaks in one layer.

2. Add tomato sauce to casserole and stir to blend. Arrange fish steaks atop the sauce and pour the lemon juice over. Bake until fish just flakes and fennel is tender, about 20 minutes. Remove fish and fennel to a warmed serving platter. Taste sauce and adjust seasoning with salt and pepper. Spoon sauce over fish and serve immediately.

Serves 4.

BACCALÀ DEL VENERDI
Friday's salt cod

A day-long soaking rids the cod of much of its salt and yields a firm-fleshed, deliciously flavored fish. Fry it quickly, then bake it slowly with tomatoes, capers, hot peppers, and lemon for a one-dish winter meal, Neapolitan style.

- 1 pound boneless salt cod
- 1 cup milk
- ⅓ cup olive oil
- 1 cup chopped onion
- 1 tablespoon minced garlic
- ½ cup flour, for dredging
- 4 cups peeled, seeded, and diced tomatoes (see page 29)
- 2 tablespoons capers
- 2 tablespoons lemon juice
- 2 tablespoons fresh oregano leaves
- ½ teaspoon hot red-pepper flakes
- 1½ pounds new red or white potatoes, in ½-inch dice
- ¼ cup freshly grated Parmesan

1. Soak cod in water to cover for 24 hours, changing water 3 or 4 times. Drain and pour milk over fish. Marinate 45 minutes. Drain and discard milk. Cut fish into four 4-ounce portions. Pat dry.

2. Heat olive oil in a heavy, stove-to-table casserole over moderate heat. Add onion and garlic and sauté 5 minutes. Dredge fish lightly in flour, shaking off excess. Brown fish on both sides in oil, about 2½ minutes on each side, and remove to a warm plate. Add tomatoes, capers, lemon juice, oregano, and pepper flakes to casserole. Simmer 5 minutes. Add fish and potatoes and simmer about 25 minutes, or until fish is very soft and potatoes are tender. Dust with Parmesan and place under a broiler to brown for 1 to 2 minutes. Serve from the dish if possible, or transfer to a warm serving bowl.

Serves 4.

GAMBERI DEL VENETO
Venetian grilled rosemary shrimp

These succulent shrimp absorb the flavors of both pre- and post-grilling marinades, emerging full of the essence of lemon, garlic, and rosemary. Serve them warm or cool, atop lettuce as a salad, or in bowls as a first course with chunks of bread to soak up the sauce.

24 large fresh shrimp, in the shell
1 cup black Calamata olives

Wine Marinade

1 cup olive oil
2 large sprigs fresh rosemary
½ cup lemon juice
2 tablespoons minced lemon rind
3 tablespoons minced garlic
¼ cup dry white wine
1 teaspoon coarse salt
1 teaspoon freshly ground black pepper

Parsley Marinade

¼ cup olive oil
2 tablespoons lemon juice
½ teaspoon coarse salt
½ teaspoon freshly ground black pepper
1 large sprig fresh rosemary
½ cup minced parsley

1. Place shrimp in a stainless steel, glass, or earthenware bowl and add Wine Marinade ingredients. Stir to blend, then cover and refrigerate 4 hours.

2. Prepare a medium-hot charcoal fire. Thread shrimp on metal skewers or on wooden skewers (soaked 1 hour in water to keep them from burning). Reserve the marinade. Grill shrimp until bright pink and barely cooked throughout. Return shrimp to bowl and add reserved Wine Marinade and all the ingredients of the Parsley Marinade. Add olives and stir well. Serve barely warm, or chill and serve the next day.

Serves 4 as a first course.

A LAKESIDE PICNIC

Scapece
(see page 14)

Gamberi del Veneto
(at left)

Legumi al Sotto
(see page 16)

Pollo alla Griglia con Aceto

Pizzette

Insalata di Patate e Cozze

Frutta e Formaggio con Dolci di Polenta

An assortment of marinated dishes makes refreshing picnic fare, especially in Indian summer weather. And all but the Little Pizzas (pizzette) can be made the night before. Bake the pizzette an hour or so before leaving; they don't need to be hot from the oven. Wrapped in plastic, they become soft and chewy and imbued with the flavor of their garnish. A chilled Verdicchio or other crisp white wine would stand up to the various marinades, but you might also want to provide some good cold beer.

POLLO ALLA GRIGLIA CON ACETO
Vinegar-marinated grilled chicken

In contrast to the usual method, this Tuscan preparation calls for the chickens to be grilled first and then marinated. As the chicken cools, it readily absorbs the tangy flavors of the marinade. Juices from the chicken and marinade will run onto a bed of lettuce, making the leaves a delectable finale.

4 chicken breast halves
Salt and freshly ground black pepper
1 head soft-leaf lettuce (butter lettuce or red leaf, for example), washed, dried, and separated into whole leaves

Vinegar Marinade

1 tablespoon grated lemon rind
2 tablespoons lemon juice
2 tablespoons dry white wine
3 tablespoons balsamic vinegar
¾ cup olive oil

1. Prepare a medium-hot charcoal fire. Season chicken with salt and pepper, then place over coals, skin side up. Brush lightly with Vinegar Marinade and grill until chicken is just done, 8 to 10 minutes on a side. Do not overcook.

2. Let chicken cool 5 minutes. If desired, remove breast bones, leaving breast halves in one piece. Put chicken in bowl along with Vinegar Marinade and continue cooling in the marinade.

3. Pack lettuce leaves and chicken in separate containers, pouring all the marinade over the chicken. Serve chicken in the center of a mound of lettuce leaves and spoon some marinade on top. Serve unboned chicken with a knife and fork. To eat boned chicken, tear off pieces of the chicken and wrap them taco-style in lettuce leaves.

Serves 4.

Vinegar Marinade In a large bowl, whisk together lemon rind, lemon juice, wine, and vinegar. Whisk in oil until thoroughly combined.

PIZZETTE
Little pizzas

A pizza topped with mozzarella or another good melting cheese should be eaten hot, before the cheese turns gummy. But a pizza that has no cheese makes a perfect snack for a picnic because it's as tasty cool as hot. By the time you've unpacked your picnic, the crust will be infused with the flavors of basil, tomato, and garlic.

> 1 recipe Basic Pizza Dough (see page 53)
> 1 tablespoon unsalted butter
> 6 tablespoons olive oil
> 1 tablespoon minced garlic
> ¾ cup minced onion
> ½ cup chopped mushrooms (optional)
> 2 tablespoons balsamic vinegar
> ¼ cup julienned fresh basil leaves
>   Cornmeal
> 1 cup seeded and diced fresh plum tomatoes (see page 29)
> 4 tablespoons freshly grated Parmesan
> 4 anchovy fillets, cut lengthwise into 4 strips each

1. Make the pizza dough through step 2 according to the directions on page 53. While dough is rising heat butter and 2 tablespoons of the oil in a medium skillet over low heat. Add garlic and onion and sauté until they are fragrant and slightly softened, about 10 minutes. If you are using mushrooms, add them to skillet after 5 minutes.

2. Turn heat to high and, when mixture begins to sizzle, add vinegar. Whisk 10 seconds and remove from heat. Stir in basil.

3. Preheat oven to 450° F. When pizza dough has doubled in volume, divide it into quarters. Roll each quarter into a small circle, about 4 to 5 inches in diameter. Dust a large, heavy baking sheet with cornmeal and transfer rounds to baking sheet. Divide onion mixture among the rounds, spreading it evenly over the surface. Garnish each round with a quarter of the tomatoes and dust each with 1 tablespoon Parmesan. Arrange anchovy strips neatly over each round. Drizzle each with one tablespoon of the remaining olive oil. Bake until bubbly, browned, and fragrant, about 12 to 16 minutes. Cool on racks, then wrap in plastic wrap.

Makes 4 little pizzas.

INSALATA DI PATATE E COZZE
Potato salad with mussels

Saffron-steamed mussels are a delicious addition to potato salad, as the cooks of Brindisi, on the "heel" of Italy, well know. They cook potatoes and mussels separately, then base the vinaigrette on the mussel cooking liquid. Sweet red peppers are a colorful but optional addition.

> 2 pounds new red potatoes
> 3 tablespoons lemon juice
> ½ cup olive oil
> 1 tablespoon coarse salt
> 6 tablespoons unsalted butter
> ½ cup minced red onion
> ½ cup dry white wine
>   Several sprigs fresh parsley
> 1 bay leaf
> 1 sprig fresh thyme
> 1 loosely packed teaspoon saffron threads
> 3 dozen mussels, well scrubbed and with beards removed (see page 67)
>   Salt and freshly ground black pepper
> ⅓ cup toasted pine nuts
> ½ cup minced green onions
> 1 bunch chives, minced
> ½ recipe Peperonata (see page 13), optional

1. Wash potatoes and put them in a large, heavy pot. Add cold salted water to come at least 2 inches above potatoes and bring to a boil over high heat. Simmer uncovered until potatoes are barely tender. Drain well. When potatoes are cool enough to handle, cut into ¾-inch dice and put them in a large bowl.

2. In a small bowl, whisk together lemon juice, olive oil, and salt until salt dissolves. Add half the mixture to the potatoes while they're still warm and toss gently to distribute dressing.

3. Melt butter in a large pot over moderate heat. Add red onion and sauté until softened, about 3 to 5 minutes. Add wine, parsley, bay leaf, thyme, and saffron. Raise heat to high and bring to a boil. Add mussels, cover, and steam until shells open, about 3 minutes, shaking pan often. Check occasionally and remove any mussels that have opened. Discard any mussels that are unopened after 3 minutes. Reserve the liquid.

4. Remove mussels from shells and discard shells. Put mussels in a small bowl and moisten with 3 tablespoons of the lemon-oil mixture. Remove parsley, bay leaf, and thyme sprig from mussel steaming liquid. Put liquid in a clean saucepan (pouring carefully to leave behind any grit) and bring to a boil over high heat. Reduce to 2 tablespoons, then remove from heat. Cool slightly, then whisk in remaining lemon-oil mixture. Season to taste with salt and pepper.

5. To the potatoes, add mussels, pine nuts, green onions, half the chives, and all remaining dressing. If using Peperonata, mix in ⅓ cup. Toss gently to blend. Taste and adjust seasoning. At the picnic site, arrange the salad in a serving bowl and garnish with the remaining chives and strips of Peperonata, if desired.

Serves 4 to 6.

FRUTTA E FORMAGGIO CON DOLCI DI POLENTA
Almond-scented fruit and ricotta with cornmeal biscuits

Juicy berries, creamy ricotta, and crisp cornmeal biscuits contrast memorably in this Piedmontese dessert. Note that the fruit must marinate at least 4 hours, and biscuit dough must chill at least 1 hour.

    2   large oranges
    3   tablespoons almond liqueur
    5   large leaves fresh mint
    1   pint raspberries
    ¼   cup blanched whole almonds
    8   ounces whole-milk ricotta
    1   tablespoon honey
    1½ tablespoons sugar
    ¼   teaspoon almond extract
        Grated rind of 1 lemon
    1   tablespoon lemon juice
    1   pint strawberries, washed,
        dried, cored, and halved

Dolci di Polenta

    1   cup cornmeal
    1¾ cups flour
    ½   teaspoon baking powder
        Pinch salt
    6   tablespoons mascarpone or
        natural cream cheese
    10 tablespoons unsalted butter,
        softened
    ½   cup sugar
    1   egg
    ½   teaspoon almond extract
    ½   teaspoon vanilla extract
    ½   cup dried currants soaked
        in 2 tablespoons Marsala
        for 1 hour

1. Grate rind of one orange and set aside. Peel both oranges and remove all white skin with a small sharp knife. Section oranges and put them in a ceramic, glass, or stainless steel bowl. Add grated orange rind, liqueur, mint, and half of the raspberries. Cover and marinate, refrigerated, at least 4 hours or overnight.

2. Preheat oven to 300° F. Toast almonds on a baking sheet until lightly browned and fragrant, about 10 minutes. Cool.

3. Put ricotta, honey, sugar, almond extract, lemon rind, lemon juice, and almonds in a food processor fitted with metal blade. Process until almonds are coarsely chopped. *Or,* chop almonds coarsely by hand, then put them in a bowl with ricotta, honey, sugar, almond extract, lemon rind, and lemon juice and stir well. Transfer mixture to a plastic container and refrigerate until departure.

4. Just before leaving for the picnic, stir strawberries and remaining raspberries into orange mixture. Transfer to a plastic container.

5. To serve, put a dollop of seasoned ricotta on each of 4 plates. Surround with marinated fruit and pass the Cornmeal Biscuits.

Serves 4.

Dolci di Polenta

1. Sift together cornmeal, flour, baking powder, and salt. Set aside.

2. *To prepare in food processor:* Put cheese and butter in processor workbowl. Process until well blended, about 5 to 8 seconds. Add sugar and process 3 seconds. Add egg, almond extract, and vanilla. Process 3 seconds. Add currants and process 3 seconds. Add flour mixture and process with on-off pulses until just mixed. *To prepare in electric mixer:* Cream the cheese and butter until blended. Add sugar and beat until light. Add egg, almond extract, and vanilla and beat until well blended. Add currants and mix to incorporate. Add flour and mix just to blend.

3. Remove dough from processor or mixer and, handling it as little as possible, form it into 2 cylinders, each 2 inches in diameter. Wrap each cylinder in plastic wrap or foil and freeze 1 hour or chill 4 to 5 hours.

4. Preheat oven to 350° F. Cut cylinders into slices ⅜ inch thick and place on greased baking sheets, leaving ½ inch between them. Bake until lightly colored, about 16 to 18 minutes. Cool on racks and store in airtight containers (biscuits will keep about a week; if they get soft, recrisp in 400° F oven for 5 minutes).

Makes about 4 dozen biscuits.

A Lakeside Picnic features grilled shrimp and chicken, marinated vegetables, mini-pizzas, potato salad, fruit, cheese, and cookies. Recipes start on page 70.

Start with a roast or a bird, combine it with the distinctive seasonings of Italy, and the result is a superb "second course" for the dinner table.

Meat & Poultry

What's for dinner? How about steak (see Bistecca alla Fiorentina, page 76), veal scaloppine (see Scaloppini di Vitello, pages 78-79), or a stew of lamb and fennel (see Spezzatino d'Agnello e Finocchi, page 81)? Or perhaps some poultry— elegant little quail in polenta nests (see Quaglie in Nidi di Polenta, page 87) or Pollo alla Diavola (see page 93)? Dishes both hearty and fancy abound in this chapter; there is also a menu for a Dinner to Honor a Fine Old Chianti (see page 90) plus instructions for preparing fennel (see page 80).

Serve Osso Buco with buttered fettuccine and a tiny spoon for scooping the soft marrow out of the veal shank bones. The hollow bone gives the dish its name.

MEAT

Italian cooks are frugal and practical connoisseurs of meat. Whether the subject is beef, veal, pork, or lamb, they know how to use every part, from the head to the tail. They braise veal shanks slowly until tender for Osso Buco (opposite page), slice expensive leg of veal into thin scallops and cook it dozens of ways (see page 78), and bring out the best in the best cuts by cooking them simply.

Simplicity and seasonality are the hallmarks of Italian meat cookery. The same basic lamb stew will incorporate tomatoes in summer, fennel in autumn, and artichokes in spring. And when the budget allows a fine piece of meat—such as a thick steak from Italy's famous Chianina beef or some young and tender lamb chops—the Italian cook's instinct is to season it simply and grill it. Dishes like Bistecca alla Fiorentina (at right) and Cotolette alla Griglia con Aglio Dolce (see page 81) reflect this innate appreciation for the simple and seasonal.

BISTECCA ALLA FIORENTINA
Florentine-style steak

The most popular dish in Florence's casual *trattorie* is a beefsteak from the local Chianina cattle. At places like Sostanza in Florence, patrons gather at long tables to enjoy what many consider the finest grilled steak in the world. A first course of minestrone and a bottle of Chianti are an important part of the ceremony.

> *Freshly ground black pepper*
> 2 *T-bone steaks (1 lb each)*
> *Kosher salt*
> *Extravirgin olive oil*
> *Cipolle al Forno (see page 22), for garnish*
> *Lemon wedges, for garnish*

Prepare a hot charcoal fire. Press ground pepper into both sides of steaks, then cook about 5 to 7 minutes per side for a rare steak, as Bistecca alla Fiorentina is traditionally served. When meat is done, salt lightly and brush with olive oil. Place on a warm serving platter and garnish with onions and lemon wedges.

Serves 4.

BRACIOLE
Rolled beef with prosciutto

Braciole is the Italian word for boneless meat cutlets, which are almost invariably stuffed, rolled, and tied. Here, in a Roman version, the cutlets are wrapped around a filling of prosciutto and celery, then gently braised with tomatoes and aromatic Italian mushrooms. Serve with a robust Italian red wine, such as a Nebbiolo d'Alba.

- *1 pound bottom round of beef*
- *⅓ pound prosciutto, sliced paper-thin*
- *1 cup coarsely chopped celery leaves*
- *3 to 4 tablespoons olive oil*
- *1 tablespoon minced garlic*
- *1 cup minced onion*
- *1½ ounces dried Italian porcini mushrooms, soaked in hot water to cover for 1 hour*
- *2 cups peeled, seeded, and diced tomatoes, fresh or canned (see page 29)*
  Salt and freshly ground black pepper

1. Have butcher slice meat into eight 2-ounce slices, or freeze it briefly and slice it yourself with a sharp knife. Place slices between two sheets of lightly oiled waxed paper and pound with a mallet or the bottom of a skillet until they are paper-thin.

2. Place beef slices on a flat surface. Divide prosciutto slices evenly among them and sprinkle chopped celery leaves over prosciutto. Roll each beef slice into a neat bundle and tie securely with kitchen string.

3. Heat 3 tablespoons oil in a heavy skillet over medium-high heat until a light haze forms. Brown beef rolls on all sides, in batches if necessary, then set aside. If necessary, add a little more oil to coat the surface of the pan, then add garlic and onion and sauté over moderate heat until softened but not browned.

4. With a slotted spoon, remove mushrooms from soaking liquid and squeeze them dry. Strain the liquid through cheesecloth to remove any grit or sand. Add mushrooms, tomatoes, and reserved soaking liquid to skillet. Season with salt and pepper to taste. Return meat to skillet and bring sauce to a simmer. Cover, reduce heat to maintain a slow simmer, and cook two hours. Check meat after 1 hour, adding a little water if sauce has reduced too much. When meat is quite tender, transfer rolls to a warm serving plate, cut the strings carefully with a small knife, and cover with the sauce.

Serves 4.

OSSO BUCO
Braised veal shanks with marrow

Meaty veal shanks turn fork-tender when braised slowly with wine and vegetables, and they yield a delectable dividend: a nugget of marrow in each "hollow bone" *(osso buco)*. Serve this Milanese classic with Risotto alla Milanese (page 61) or surrounded by lightly buttered fettuccine:

- *3 veal shanks, each sawed into 6 to 8 pieces about 2½ inches long*
  Salt and freshly ground black pepper
- *2 cups flour, for dredging*
- *½ to ¾ cup safflower oil*
- *1¼ cups dry white wine*
- *2 cups veal stock or beef stock (if using canned beef stock, dilute with water to taste, to reduce strength and saltiness)*
- *4 sprigs fresh thyme*
- *½ cup parsley sprigs and stems*
- *3 bay leaves*
- *1 cup whole fresh basil leaves*
- *5 tablespoons butter*
- *1½ cups chopped onion*
- *1 cup diced celery*
- *1 cup diced carrot*
- *1 tablespoon minced garlic*
- *2 cups peeled, seeded, and chopped tomatoes (see page 29)*

Gremolata

- *2 tablespoons finely minced Italian parsley*
- *1 tablespoon grated lemon rind*
- *1 teaspoon finely minced garlic*

1. Salt and pepper the shanks well, then dredge them lightly in flour and shake off excess. In a large Dutch oven over medium-high heat, heat oil. Add shanks and brown them well on all sides, in batches if necessary. Transfer shanks to a plate as they are browned.

2. When all the shanks have been browned, add wine to Dutch oven and bring to a boil. With a wooden spoon, scrape up any browned bits clinging to the bottom of pot. Add stock and simmer 2 minutes.

3. Place thyme, parsley, and bay leaves in a cheesecloth bag. Add to pot along with basil. Return shanks to pot and set aside.

4. In a large skillet over moderate heat, melt butter. Add onion, celery, carrot, and garlic and cook until vegetables are slightly softened, about 5 minutes. Add tomatoes and simmer 5 minutes. Transfer mixture to Dutch oven, cover tightly, and bring to a simmer over moderately high heat. Reduce heat to maintain simmer and cook gently for at least 2 hours. (The dish may also be baked in a 325° F oven for 2½ to 3 hours; bring it to a simmer on top of stove first.) Check occasionally to make sure liquid has not reduced too much; add a little wine, stock, or water if necessary.

5. When meat is fork-tender, transfer the shanks to a warm serving platter. Place the pot briefly over high heat to reduce sauce slightly. Add Gremolata during final 30 seconds, then spoon the sauce over the meat.

Serves 8.

Gremolata Combine parsley, lemon rind, and garlic in a small bowl.

MAIALE CON FAVE, CIPOLLE, E POMODORI
Tenderloin of pork with fava beans, onions, and tomatoes

For this Umbrian dish, season pork medallions in a lemon marinade overnight, then grill them quickly over charcoal for informal summer parties. Accompany with grilled onions and a relish made from vine-ripened tomatoes; if your grill is large enough, include a platter of Polenta alla Griglia (see page 59).

- 2½ pounds pork loin
- ½ cup olive oil
- 2 tablespoons lemon juice
- 1 tablespoon grated lemon rind
- 2 tablespoons minced garlic
- ¼ cup fresh basil leaves
- 3 cups onion, slices, ¼ inch thick (do not separate into rings)
- 2 cups peeled, seeded, and chopped fresh tomatoes (see page 29)
- ⅓ cup minced parsley
- 2 tablespoons minced shallot
- 2 tablespoons minced chives
- 2 tablespoons balsamic vinegar
  Salt, to taste

1. Have butcher cut loin into 12 medallions about ½ inch thick (or cut them yourself). Pound them lightly with a mallet or the back of skillet.

2. Whisk together ¼ cup olive oil, the lemon juice, lemon rind, garlic, and basil. Put pork medallions and onion slices in a glass, ceramic, or stainless steel container; pour olive oil mixture over them. Cover and marinate, refrigerated, at least 4 hours or up to 12 hours.

3. Prepare relish by combining tomatoes, the remaining olive oil, the parsley, shallot, chives, and vinegar, and salt to taste. Set aside.

4. Remove meat from refrigerator about 1 hour before grilling. Prepare a medium-hot charcoal fire. Remove onions from marinade, pat dry, and grill briefly, until charred but still crunchy. Set aside and spoon some of the marinade over them. Grill the pork quickly on both sides, until just cooked through. Serve the pork hot off the grill, with a spoonful of tomato relish on top and grilled onions alongside.

Serves 6.

Make-Ahead Tip The tomato relish may be made a day ahead, covered, and refrigerated, but wait to add salt until just before serving. Bring relish to room temperature before serving.

SCALOPPINE DI VITELLO
Veal scaloppine

Use milk-fed veal from the leg for these quick sautés. When pounded to an even ⅛-inch thickness, the little scallops (scaloppine) cook through quickly and remain tender. You probably won't want to attempt scaloppine for large parties; even dinner for four requires two skillets and two burners. However, the technique is easy and quick, and many garnishes can be prepared ahead. Veal scaloppine are extremely versatile and can be prepared with dozens of different sauces and garnishes; three possibilities are given here. The lemon-sauce recipe is from Venice, the porcini-and-Marsala from Piedmont, and the basil-butter version from Genoa.

- ¾ pound leg of veal, cut into six 2-ounce scallops
  Salt and freshly ground black pepper
- ½ cup flour for dredging
- 2 tablespoons unsalted butter
- 2 tablespoons olive oil

Salt and pepper veal lightly. Dredge veal lightly in flour, shaking off excess. Arrange veal slices on a plate near your stove top. In each of two large skillets, heat 1 tablespoon of the butter and 1 tablespoon of the oil over moderately high heat. When mixture foams add three scallops to each pan. Do not crowd scallops. Brown meat quickly on both sides (about 30 seconds per side), then transfer to warmed plates and serve immediately.

Serves 2 to 3.

Scaloppine al Limone
Sweet-and-sour lemon sauce

- ¼ cup dry white wine
- 1 tablespoon water
- 1½ tablespoons sugar
- 1 teaspoon honey
- 1 lemon, seeded and sliced paper-thin
- 2 tablespoons minced shallots
- 3 tablespoons lemon juice plus additional to taste
- 4 tablespoons unsalted butter, softened
- 1 tablespoon minced parsley
  Freshly ground black pepper

1. Place wine, water, sugar, and honey in a nonaluminum saucepan and bring to a boil. Add lemon slices and simmer gently for 10 minutes, or until slices are translucent. Remove lemons from syrup and continue cooking until syrup is reduced to about ½ cup. Return lemon slices to syrup and set aside.

2. Sauté veal as directed above, reducing cooking time to 15 to 20 seconds on each side (they will finish cooking in the sauce). Use at least one nonaluminum skillet. Transfer cooked veal to a plate. Consolidate any juices and browned bits in nonaluminum skillet, add shallots, and sauté until almost golden, about 3 minutes. Add lemon juice, then swirl in butter to thicken. Add 2 tablespoons reduced lemon syrup.

Taste and add up to 2 teaspoons more lemon juice, if desired. Return veal to skillet just to heat through, then divide scallops and sauce among warmed dinner plates. Arrange two slices of cooked lemon on each plate and sprinkle veal with parsley and black pepper.

Make-Ahead Tip Sweet-and-sour lemon sauce may be made up to 3 hours ahead and stored, covered, in refrigerator. Warm sauce before placing scallops in it.

Scaloppine con Porcini e Marsala
Porcini and Marsala sauce

- 1 *ounce dried Italian porcini mushrooms*
- 1 *cup warm water*
- 4 *tablespoons unsalted butter*
- 2 *tablespoons finely minced garlic*
- ¼ *cup Marsala*
  Salt and freshly ground black pepper
  Minced parsley

1. Soak porcini in the warm water for 30 minutes. Drain, reserving liquid. Strain liquid through a double thickness of cheesecloth to remove any sand or dirt. Dry mushrooms, inspecting them closely for dirt or grit, and slice thinly.

2. Sauté veal as directed on opposite page, reducing cooking time to 15 to 20 seconds on each side (they will finish cooking in the sauce). Transfer cooked veal to a plate. To one of the skillets used to sauté veal, add 1 tablespoon butter and the garlic. Sauté until fragrant, then add mushrooms, Marsala, and ½ cup reserved mushroom liquid. Bring to a boil and reduce until about ½ cup remains. Remove pan from heat and swirl in remaining butter, cut into small pieces. Season to taste with salt and pepper. Return veal to pan briefly just to warm through. Divide scallops and sauce among warmed dinner plates. Garnish with minced parsley.

Scaloppine alla Genovese
Basil butter with pine nuts

- 4 *tablespoons unsalted butter, softened*
- 1 *tablespoon olive oil*
- ½ *cup fresh basil leaves*
- 1 *teaspoon finely minced garlic*
  Salt and freshly ground black pepper
- 2 *tablespoons pine nuts*
- 2 *tablespoons freshly grated Parmesan*

1. Preheat oven to 375° F. In a blender or food processor, combine butter, oil, basil, garlic, and salt and pepper to taste. Blend until smooth; set aside. Toast pine nuts in oven on a rimmed baking sheet, shaking it often, until fragrant and lightly colored, about 7 minutes.

2. Sauté veal as directed above. Transfer veal to warmed dinner plates. Top each portion with a dollop of basil butter, a few toasted pine nuts, and a dusting of Parmesan.

Scaloppine alla Genovese shows fork-tender scaloppine at its simplest and best, with a fragrant basil butter and pine nuts.

PREPARING FENNEL

1. *Cut off and discard fennel tops; remove bruised or discolored outer ribs; trim base.*

2. *Halve bulbs and core them.*

3. *Slice thinly lengthwise.*

SPEZZATINO DI CONIGLIO CON POLENTA
Rabbit stew with baked polenta

Slow braising with wine and herbs brings out the best in storebought rabbit. Here it's simmered until fork-tender, then sauced with capers, anchovies, and cream. Baked Polenta is served alongside to absorb the sauce. Serve this full-flavored Venetian dish in the fall or winter with a similarly full-flavored wine—a Barbaresco or an Italian Merlot.

 3 tablespoons butter
 3 tablespoons (approximately) olive oil
 2 large rabbits (about 3 lb each), cut into serving pieces
 1½ cups (approximately) flour, for dredging
 ¼ cup brandy
 1 cup diced pancetta
 4 cups sliced onion
 2 tablespoons minced garlic
 2 tablespoons flour
 1 small sprig fresh rosemary or 1 teaspoon dried rosemary
 A few fresh sage leaves
 1 teaspoon fresh tarragon leaves or ½ teaspoon dried tarragon
 6 fresh oregano sprigs
 2 cups dry white wine
 1 cup cream
 2 anchovy fillets, mashed to a paste
 1 tablespoon capers
 Salt and freshly ground black pepper
 Fresh parsley sprigs, for garnish

Baked Polenta

 1 cup water
 3 cups milk
 1 teaspoon salt
 12 tablespoons unsalted butter
 1 cup polenta
 ¼ cup flour
 1¼ cups freshly grated Parmesan
 2 egg yolks

1. Preheat oven to 350° F. Heat butter and oil in an ovenproof skillet over moderately high heat. Dredge rabbit pieces lightly in flour, shaking off excess. Brown well on all sides, in batches if necessary. Add brandy to last batch and carefully flame with a long match. When flames die down, remove rabbit to a plate.

2. Add pancetta, onions, and garlic to fat in skillet. Sauté gently until onions are golden and pancetta is crisp, about 15 minutes. (Add more olive oil if necessary to keep pancetta from sticking.) Add flour and cook, stirring, 5 minutes. Add rosemary, sage, tarragon, oregano, and wine. Stir with a wooden spoon to loosen browned bits from bottom of skillet. Return rabbit pieces to skillet. Bring to a simmer, cover with lid or foil, and transfer to oven. Cook 1¼ to 1½ hours, or until fork-tender.

3. Remove rabbit to a warmed serving platter and cover with foil to keep warm. Pour sauce into a cup and let fat rise to the top. Spoon off fat, then return liquid to a small clean saucepan. Reduce liquid by half over high heat. Whisk in cream, anchovy paste, and capers. Taste and adjust seasoning as necessary.

4. Pour anchovy sauce over rabbit pieces on serving platter, surround with Baked Polenta, and serve immediately.

Serves 8.

Baked Polenta

1. In a heavy, medium saucepan over moderate heat, combine water and milk with salt and 2 tablespoons of the butter. Bring to a boil, then gradually whisk in polenta and flour. Continue whisking until mixture thickens slightly, then switch to a wooden spoon and cook, stirring constantly, until mixture is smooth and thick, about 20 minutes. Stir in 6 tablespoons more butter and cook an additional 5 minutes, stirring often. Remove polenta from heat and stir in half the cheese and the two egg yolks. Pour polenta onto a buttered 9- by 11- by 1½-inch roasting pan. Cool.

2. Twenty-five minutes before the rabbit is done, cut cooled polenta into desired shapes (rounds, hearts, diamonds, squares, for example). Place on a buttered baking sheet. Dot with remaining butter; sprinkle with remaining cheese. Place in oven alongside the rabbit and cook 15 minutes. After removing rabbit from the oven, turn heat up to 450° F and brown the polenta.

Serves 8.

COTOLETTE ALLA GRIGLIA CON AGLIO DOLCE
Grilled lamb chops with sweet garlic

To grill the most aromatic lamb chops ever, toss lemon branches or leaves or fresh rosemary sprigs on top of the hot coals. A lemon marinade adds even more character to this Tuscan lamb; sweet stewed garlic and hot tomato-topped bread are the perfect accompaniments. Serve with a cool Italian Merlot, and end the meal with homemade ice cream.

- 12 *small loin lamb chops*
- 1 *small white onion, minced*
- ¼ *cup dry white wine*
- ¼ *cup lemon juice*
- 1 *tablespoon finely minced lemon rind*
- 1 *pound whole garlic cloves, unpeeled*
- 11 *tablespoons olive oil*
  One 10-inch round loaf (or equivalent) of day-old, country-style bread, preferably homemade
- 2 *cups peeled, seeded, and chopped tomatoes (see page 29)*
  Salt and freshly ground black pepper
  Lemon branches or leaves or fresh rosemary sprigs
- 2 *tablespoons melted butter mixed with 1 tablespoon olive oil*
- ¼ *cup minced parsley*
  Freshly grated Parmesan

1. Put lamb chops in a glass, ceramic, or stainless steel container. Make a marinade by combining onion, white wine, lemon juice, and lemon rind in a bowl. Pour over chops and marinate 2 hours at room temperature.

2. Put garlic and 3 tablespoons olive oil in a saucepan. Add water just to cover. Bring to a simmer, reduce heat, cover, and simmer until garlic is very soft (45 minutes to 1 hour). Drain and reserve garlic.

3. Cut bread into slices about ½ inch thick. Combine tomatoes, remaining olive oil, and salt and pepper to taste and let steep 30 minutes. Spread a little tomato mixture on each slice of bread, stacking bread slices as you go. Wrap slices, re-formed in loaf shape, in foil and set aside.

4. Prepare a medium-hot charcoal fire. When coals are ready, place lemon branches or leaves or rosemary sprigs on them. When flames die down, grill chops to desired doneness. Brush garlic cloves with butter-oil mixture, wrap in foil, and reheat on top of the grill. If you have room underneath the grate, tuck foil-wrapped bread in with the coals to reheat. Otherwise, preheat oven to 350° F and reheat bread for 15 minutes.

5. To serve, arrange chops in the center of a large platter. Surround with slices of tomato-scented bread sprinkled with parsley. Salt the garlic cloves and scatter them around the platter. Pass Parmesan at the table to sprinkle on the bread.

Serves 6.

SPEZZATINO D'AGNELLO E FINOCCHI
Lamb and fennel stew

Look for fennel in autumn and winter and enjoy its licorice flavor as the Italians do: in soups and salads, with fish and pork, and in lamb stews like this Roman one. Like most stews, it can easily be made ahead and reheated. If fennel is unobtainable, choose another lamb dish, such as Agnello con Carciofi or Agnello con Acciughe e Caperi (both on page 82).

- ¾ *cup olive oil*
- 2½ *pounds lamb shoulder, in 2-inch cubes*
- 1 *cup thinly sliced red onion*
- 1 *tablespoon coarse salt*
- 2 *teaspoons freshly ground black pepper*
- ¾ *cup dry white wine*
- 6 *small fennel bulbs, well trimmed and halved, or 3 large bulbs, quartered (opposite page)*
- 2 *tablespoons minced garlic*
- 2 *tablespoons balsamic vinegar*

1. Preheat oven to 350° F. Heat ½ cup of the oil in a large skillet and brown lamb on all sides, in batches if necessary. Transfer browned lamb to a large, flameproof casserole.

2. Add onions to skillet and sauté until softened, about 5 minutes. Add to lamb in casserole along with salt and pepper. Add wine to the skillet and bring to a boil. Use a wooden spoon to scrape up any browned bits clinging to the bottom. Add wine to casserole. Bring contents of casserole to a simmer on top of the stove, then cover and place in oven.

3. Heat remaining olive oil in a large skillet until hot but not smoking. Add fennel and brown on all sides. Transfer browned fennel to a plate and add garlic to skillet. Sauté just until fragrant. Pour vinegar into skillet and bring to a boil, stirring with a wooden spoon to scrape up any browned bits. Pour over fennel. If fennel is large, add fennel-garlic mixture to casserole when lamb has cooked 1 hour. If it is young and small, add it when lamb has cooked 1½ hours. Continue braising until lamb is fork-tender, a total of about 2 to 2½ hours.

4. When meat tests done, transfer meat and fennel pieces to a warmed serving platter with a slotted spoon. If braising juices are too thin, reduce them over high heat, then spoon them over the stew.

Serves 6.

AGNELLO CON ACCIUGHE E CAPERI
Leg of lamb with anchovies and capers

Easy to carve, a boned and butterflied leg of lamb cooks quickly on a charcoal grill (it can also be roasted in the oven). This recipe features both a marinade of anchovies, garlic, and wine, which adds a southern Italian flavor, and a tangy anchovy-caper sauce. Leftovers make memorable sandwiches.

  2 *tins (2 oz* each*) anchovy fillets*
  2 *tablespoons minced garlic*
  1 *leg of lamb, boned and butterflied*
  ¼ *cup olive oil*
  ¾ *cup red wine*
  ¼ *cup lemon juice*
  3 *sprigs fresh rosemary*
  1 *cup mixed fresh herbs (basil, thyme, oregano)*
    Salt and freshly ground black pepper
  4 *ounces unsalted butter*
  ½ *cup capers*
  2 *tablespoons lemon juice*

1. Purée 2 ounces of the anchovies with garlic in a food processor or mortar. Lay butterflied lamb out flat and spread anchovy paste over the underside. Whisk together olive oil, wine, and lemon juice. Put lamb, paste side up, in a glass, ceramic, or stainless steel container along with rosemary and mixed herbs, and pour the olive oil mixture over. Cover and marinate overnight. Bring the lamb to room temperature before continuing.

2. *To grill:* Prepare a medium-hot charcoal fire. Season lamb with salt and pepper. Place lamb paste side down on grill; grill, covered, until internal temperature reaches 120° F to 125° F for rare, 25 to 30 minutes. If fire is very hot, check lamb after about 15 minutes; it will cook quickly. *To roast in oven:* Preheat oven to 350° F. Season lamb with salt and pepper. Roast lamb paste side down until internal temperature reaches 120° F to 125° F for rare, 25 to 30 minutes. Let rest 10 minutes before slicing.

3. To make caper sauce: Heat butter in a skillet. Add the remaining anchovies and mash with the back of a wooden spoon. Heat through gently, then add capers and lemon juice.

4. To serve, slice lamb thinly against the grain and transfer to warmed platter. Spoon caper sauce over lamb or serve it on the side.

Serves 6.

AGNELLO CON CARCIOFI
Lamb with artichokes

This rustic dish from Empoli is best presented family-style: Arrange the sage-scented chops in the center of a large platter and surround with braised artichokes and prosciutto on toast. Fresh sage and a good, dense bread are essential ingredients.

  1 *lemon*
  3 *small fresh artichokes, no larger than 1½ inches in diameter*
  ¼ *pound prosciutto, in one piece*
  3 *tablespoons olive oil (more if necessary)*
  2 *tablespoons unsalted butter*
  6 *loin lamb chops, thick-cut*
  ⅓ *cup fresh whole sage leaves*
  ⅓ *cup Marsala*
  6 *thick slices toasted country-style bread, preferably homemade*
  3 *tablespoons minced parsley, for garnish*

1. Squeeze juice from lemon into a small bowl filled with water. Prepare artichokes according to the directions on page 16. Quarter artichokes and remove any fuzzy chokes. Drop artichokes into the bowl of lemon juice and water.

2. Cut prosciutto into small dice. Heat 1 tablespoon olive oil in a skillet over medium-low heat, add prosciutto, and sauté until brown. Drain and dry artichokes; add to skillet and sauté over medium-low heat until tender, 10 to 15 minutes, adding more oil if necessary. Transfer prosciutto and artichokes to a plate; keep warm.

3. Put 1 tablespoon oil and 1 tablespoon butter in each of two skillets. Brown chops quickly on both sides over high heat. Add half the sage leaves and half the Marsala to each skillet and cook until lamb is done to your liking, adjusting heat to keep Marsala from boiling away. Remove chops to a warm serving platter and surround them with toasts. Put all the juices in one skillet along with the artichokes and prosciutto. Reduce slightly over high heat to glaze artichokes, then arrange them over toast and garnish with parsley.

Serves 3 to 4.

SALSICCE CON PEPERONI MISTI E POLENTA
Sausage with mixed peppers and polenta

Plump sausage and golden polenta make a rib-sticking family supper or a colorful dish for casual entertaining. If you have a large platter, serve this Venetian dish family-style: Make a foundation of polenta, then arrange the browned sausages and sautéed peppers on top. To complete the meal, add a Barbera or a simple Chianti and a light fruit dessert.

  4 *hot Italian pork sausages*
  4 *sweet Italian pork sausages with fennel*
  ½ *cup dry white wine*
  ½ *cup olive oil*
  3 *tablespoons minced garlic*
  1 *cup coarsely chopped green bell pepper*
  1 *cup coarsely chopped red bell pepper*
  1 *cup coarsely chopped yellow bell pepper (or substitute an additional ½ cup each green and red pepper)*
  ½ *cup thinly sliced red onion*
  ¼ *cup fresh oregano leaves*
    Salt, to taste

Creamy Polenta

  4 *cups water*
  1 *tablespoon salt*
  3 *tablespoons unsalted butter*
  1 *cup polenta*
  ¾ *cup whipping cream*
  ½ *cup freshly grated Parmesan*

1. Prick sausages all over with a fork and place in a lidded sauté pan (no fat or liquid is needed). Brown over high heat on all sides. Turn down heat and add wine carefully (it will sputter). Cover pan, and poach sausages gently until done, about 10 minutes.

2. While sausages are cooking, heat olive oil in a separate skillet over moderate heat. Add garlic and sauté until fragrant. Add peppers, onions, and oregano and sauté, stirring often, until slightly softened, about 5 minutes. Add salt to taste.

3. To serve, divide polenta among warm serving plates. Top with sautéed peppers and place one of each kind of sausage alongside.

Serves 4.

Creamy Polenta In a large saucepan with a heavy bottom over high heat, bring water, salt, and 1 tablespoon butter to a boil. Slowly whisk in polenta in a steady stream until mixture is smooth. Cook, stirring often with a wooden spoon, for 10 minutes. Add cream and cook, stirring often, until mixture is thick and creamy and tastes fully cooked, about 10 minutes more. Stir in remaining butter and cheese and keep warm until ready to serve.

Serves 4.

Salsicce con Peperoni Misti e Polenta combines sausage with peppers and polenta in a Venetian dish for hearty appetites. Its vivid colors and rustic flavors would suit an informal dinner for friends. Steamed greens, such as the red chard shown here, would make a good side dish.

Garlic, rosemary, and hot-pepper flakes add zest to a Sicilian-style pork roast. Serve Arrosto di Maiale con Rosmarino with sautéed greens and a light red wine.

SALTIMBOCCA
Veal scallops with prosciutto and sage

This Roman dish is a good example of the Italian penchant for whimsical food names; it is so succulent it almost leaps into your mouth *(salta in bocca)*. The success of the dish depends on tender, milk-fed veal and fresh sage. Serve with a light red wine or a rich Italian Chardonnay.

  1¼ *pounds leg of veal, cut into 12 scallops*
      Salt and freshly ground black pepper
  12 *fresh sage leaves*
  12 *paper-thin slices prosciutto*
   2 *tablespoons unsalted butter*
   3 *tablespoons dry white wine*
  1½ *tablespoons minced parsley*

1. Place each scallop between pieces of oiled waxed paper and, using a mallet or the bottom of a skillet, pound to a uniform ⅛-inch thickness. Salt and pepper scallops lightly. Put a sage leaf on each and cover with a slice of prosciutto. Secure prosciutto to scallop with toothpicks.

2. Melt 1 tablespoon of the butter in each of two large skillets. Add scal-

lops and brown quickly on both sides. When scallops are just barely cooked, transfer them to a warmed serving platter; remove toothpicks. Scrape juices and browned bits from one skillet to the other. Add the wine to the skillet with the juices and reduce slightly over high heat. Pour sauce over scallops; garnish with parsley.

Serves 4.

ARROSTO DI MAIALE CON ROSMARINO
Sicilian-style pork roast with rosemary

This well-seasoned pork roast appears on Sunday lunch tables all over Italy, usually preceded by a soup or pasta and accompanied by sautéed greens. In Florence it's rubbed with rosemary or fennel and called *arista* (the best); Sicilian cooks add garlic and hot-pepper flakes.

  2 *tablespoons minced garlic*
  1 *tablespoon grated lemon rind*
  1 *teaspoon hot red-pepper flakes*
  2 *teaspoons salt*
  5 *pounds boneless pork rib roast, untied*
  3 *tablespoons olive oil*
  1 *tablespoon freshly ground black pepper*
  5 *sprigs fresh rosemary*

1. Preheat oven to 350° F. Put garlic, lemon rind, hot-pepper flakes, and 1 teaspoon salt in food processor or blender. Process to a paste. Set aside 1½ teaspoons paste and rub the remainder into the underside of the meat. Tie the roast neatly with string. Using a small, sharp knife, make four incisions, about ½ inch long and ½ inch deep, in the roast. Stuff the incisions with the remaining paste. Rub roast all over with olive oil, then with black pepper and remaining teaspoon of salt. Tie the rosemary sprigs onto the roast with string.

2. Place roast on a rack in a roasting pan and roast 2 to 2½ hours, or until a meat thermometer registers 145° F. Remove and let rest 10 minutes before slicing.

Serves 8.

ARROSTO DI MAIALE AL LATTE
Pork loin in milk

The idea may sound odd to Americans, but pork pot-roasted in milk is a much-loved Tuscan dish. The milk cooks down into rich, nutty clumps that are what the Italians call *bruti ma buoni* (ugly but good). Serve the roast with wilted chard or spinach and a light Chianti.

> 1 tablespoon unsalted butter
> 2 tablespoons olive oil
> 1½ pounds boneless pork loin, neatly tied to hold its shape
> 2 cups milk
> ½ cup half-and-half
> Salt and freshly ground black pepper
> 2 sprigs fresh rosemary (optional)
> 1 bay leaf
> ½ pound pearl onions, peeled and parboiled 5 minutes
> 2 tablespoons minced parsley

1. In a Dutch oven just large enough to hold the pork, melt butter and oil over moderately high heat. Add meat and brown well on all sides.

2. In a separate pot, scald milk and half-and-half. Add to browned meat along with salt and pepper to taste, rosemary (if used), and bay leaf. Bring to a simmer, cover, and reduce heat to maintain a steady simmer. Braise 1½ hours, or until meat is tender when pierced with a knife. Add onions about 15 minutes before meat is done. If milk is still runny, remove meat and keep warm; put Dutch oven over high heat and reduce milk till brown clumps form, whisking occasionally.

3. After meat has rested 10 minutes, remove string and slice with a long, sharp knife. Arrange slices on a warmed serving platter and scatter the onions around. Spoon the sauce over the meat and garnish with minced parsley.

Serves 4.

POULTRY

"Poultry" in Italy means quite a bit more than just the ubiquitous chicken. Italians are enthusiastic eaters of duck, squab, quail, and other wild birds large and small. They love them grilled or spit-roasted (especially popular in restaurants), braised in the oven, stewed in sauce, or simply baked with garden herbs. The collection that follows is just a hint of this extensive repertoire. Pollo alla Griglia con Salsa d'Aglio (see page 95) and Gambe d'Anitra alla Griglia (see page 93) are typical of dishes suited to casual, warm-weather dinners; more formal, sit-down meals might feature Pollo Novello alla Cacciatora (see page 89) or Quaglie in Nidi di Polenta (see page 87). For best results, buy freshly killed poultry that has not been frozen.

FETE DI POLLO CON PIGNOLI E LIMONE
Grilled chicken "steaks" with pine nut and lemon sauce

Boned and flattened chicken breasts can be quickly pan-fried and served with any of the sauces or garnishes used for Scallopine di Vitello (see pages 78–79). In this Tuscan dish, a light and lemony sauce enriched with ground pine nuts is made in minutes with a chicken stock reduction. Barely wilted spinach or chard is a good accompaniment.

> 4 whole chicken breasts, split and boned
> 3 cups chicken stock
> 1 cup dry white wine
> ½ cup minced carrot
> ½ cup minced onion
> 2 tablespoons white wine vinegar
> Pinch hot red-pepper flakes
> Grated rind of 1 lemon
> Salt
> 3 tablespoons butter
> 3 tablespoons olive oil
> ¼ cup toasted and finely ground pine nuts
> 2 tablespoons lemon juice
> 2 tablespoons minced Italian parsley
> 2 tablespoons toasted pine nuts, for garnish

1. Pound chicken breasts between two pieces of oiled waxed paper to ¼-inch thickness. Put stock, wine, carrot, onion, vinegar, pepper flakes, and lemon rind in a nonaluminum saucepan and bring to a boil. Simmer uncovered until sauce is reduced to about 2 cups (about 1 hour). Strain through a sieve; taste and add salt if necessary.

2. Heat two large skillets over moderately high heat. Divide butter and oil between them; when butter foams, add chicken and sauté quickly, about 45 to 60 seconds per side. Remove chicken to a warm serving platter and keep in a warm oven while you finish the sauce.

3. Bring chicken stock mixture to a boil and whisk in ground pine nuts, lemon juice, and 1 tablespoon parsley. Pour sauce over chicken and garnish with whole pine nuts and remaining parsley.

Serves 8.

Plump sausage-stuffed quail in polenta "nests" are a dish for a fancy dinner party. Accompany Quaglie in Nidi di Polenta with a fine red wine.

ALI DI POLLO CON PANCETTA
Chicken wings with pancetta

Knives and forks can't possibly get to the good parts on chicken wings. Fingers are the best utensils, and big napkins or bibs are a must. If you have a stove-to-table casserole, serve this colorful Modenese dish country-style, with some good, crusty bread to soak up the tomato and saffron sauce.

- ¼ pound pancetta, in one piece
- ¾ cup unbleached flour
- 1 teaspoon freshly ground black pepper
- 2 teaspoons salt
- 2 pounds chicken wings, wing tips removed
- 2 tablespoons butter
- 1½ teaspoons olive oil
- ½ cup minced onion
- 2 tablespoons minced green onion
- 1½ teaspoons minced garlic
- 2 sprigs fresh oregano, leaves only, or 1 teaspoon dried oregano
- ½ cup dry white wine
- ½ teaspoon saffron threads softened in 2 teaspoons warm water; reserve liquid
- 2 cups coarsely chopped mushrooms
- 1 cup peeled, seeded, and chopped fresh tomatoes (see page 29) or ½ cup Sugo di Pomodoro (see page 36)
- ½ cup chicken stock
  Salt and freshly ground black pepper
- 2 tablespoons minced parsley, for garnish

1. Dice pancetta, then render slowly in a large frying pan until crisp. Transfer with a slotted spoon to paper towels to drain, leaving fat in pan.

2. Combine flour, black pepper, and salt in a paper bag. Dredge wings lightly in flour mixture, shaking off excess. Add butter and olive oil to pancetta fat in skillet. Brown wings in fat over moderately high heat. Remove them to a plate when they are brown all over.

3. Add onion, green onion, garlic, and oregano to skillet and cook slowly for 10 minutes. Return wings to skillet; add wine, saffron, and saffron-soaking liquid to skillet. Cook 5 minutes over medium heat. The mixture should reduce slightly.

4. Add mushrooms, tomatoes, and stock to skillet. Cover and simmer 25 minutes or until wings are tender. Add rendered pancetta and cook uncovered for about 5 minutes to reduce the sauce slightly. Season to taste with salt and pepper. Transfer to a warmed serving bowl or platter and garnish with minced parsley.

Serves 3 to 4.

QUAGLIE IN NIDI DI POLENTA
Stuffed quail in polenta cups

Cut into these tender quail to reveal a juicy sausage stuffing, made in minutes using storebought fennel sausage. The dark-breasted birds make a rich autumn entrée that stands up to a Gattinara or a stately Chianti Classico Riserva. Surround the quail with hot polenta (see page 58) if you prefer, but the nestlike cups make a particularly charming presentation. The recipe is from Venice.

- ⅔ pound fresh sweet Italian pork sausages with fennel, casing removed
- ¼ cup freshly grated Romano
- 2 tablespoons lemon juice
- 1 tablespoon minced garlic (optional)
- 8 quail
  Salt and freshly ground black pepper
- 3 tablespoons unsalted butter
- 1 tablespoon olive oil
- 2 tablespoons white wine

Polenta Cups

- 1 recipe Basic Polenta (see page 58)
  Butter, to grease dishes

1. Make stuffing by crumbling sausage and frying it slowly in a skillet until it is no longer pink. Remove with slotted spoon to a bowl and cool slightly. Stir cheese and lemon juice into sausage. If sausage is not already highly seasoned with garlic, add the 1 tablespoon minced garlic. Set stuffing aside.

2. Preheat oven to 450° F. Season quail generously with salt and pepper. Place half the butter and half the oil in a large skillet over medium-high heat; heat until butter melts. Brown birds quickly, in batches if necessary. Transfer to a plate and cool slightly. Stuff birds loosely with stuffing mixture. Reserve any remaining stuffing.

3. Place remaining oil and butter in a small skillet over low heat; heat until butter melts. Remove from heat and add wine. Brush quail all over with this mixture. Transfer quail to a roasting pan and roast breast side up, basting occasionally with wine-butter mixture, for 10 to 12 minutes. Quail should be nicely browned, and legs should move freely. Arrange each quail in a Polenta Cup, on top of any extra stuffing. Serve immediately.

Serves 8 as a first course or 4 as a main course.

Polenta Cups Preheat oven to 400° F. Spoon still-warm polenta into buttered 1½-cup soufflé dishes, custard cups, or 3-inch tartlet pans with removable bottoms. As polenta cools, push it up the sides of the dish to form a cup shape. Cool completely. Bake cups 10 minutes. Cool and remove from dishes.

POLLO CON PORCINI
Porcini roast chicken

Stuff a plump chicken with aromatic *porcini* mushrooms, then use the mushroom stuffing to make a simple, last-minute sauce. Serve this Parma-style chicken with Creamy Polenta (see page 82) and a Nebbiolo d'Alba.

- 1½ ounces dried Italian porcini mushrooms
- 1 tablespoon rendered chicken fat
- 2 tablespoons olive oil
- 3 tablespoons butter
- 1 tablespoon minced garlic
  Chicken liver and heart, minced
- ½ pound mushrooms, minced
- 1 tablespoon Marsala
  Salt and freshly ground black pepper
- 1 roasting chicken (about 4 lb)
- 1 lemon
- 1 cup less 2 tablespoons chicken stock
  Fresh parsley sprigs or watercress, for garnish

1. Soak porcini in warm water to cover for 30 minutes. Lift them out with a slotted spoon and check them carefully for grit. Slice thinly. Strain liquid through a double thickness of cheesecloth and set aside.

2. Heat chicken fat, olive oil, and butter in a large skillet over moderately low heat. Add garlic and sauté slowly for 3 minutes. Add chicken liver and heart and sauté 3 minutes. Add mushrooms and porcini and cook an additional 3 minutes. Add Marsala and cook 2 minutes. Remove from heat and season to taste with salt and pepper.

3. Preheat oven to 325° F. Dry chicken thoroughly inside and out. Stuff cavity with mushroom mixture. Truss the chicken. Squeeze the lemon over the top and lightly salt and pepper the outside. Place on a rack in a roasting pan and roast breast side down for 45 minutes, basting occasionally with drippings. Turn chicken

over and roast until the juices run clear. When chicken is done, place it under broiler for 1 to 2 minutes, or until the skin is crisp and golden. Remove from broiler and let rest 5 minutes.

4. While chicken is resting, bring chicken stock and 2 tablespoons porcini liquid to a boil in a saucepan and reduce to ½ cup. Turn heat to low while chicken is being carved. Add stuffing to the sauce, blend well, and pour over chicken. Garnish platter with parsley or watercress.

Serves 3 to 4.

FAGOTINI DI POLLO CON CIPOLLE BALSAMICHE
Chicken livers with balsamic onions

Grilled sage-scented poultry livers served with sweet-and-sour onions are a delightful variation on the liver-and-onions theme. With chunks of country bread, guests can make their own *crostini*, piling livers and onions on top to make a juicy mouthful. In smaller portions, this dish from Modena makes a fine appetizer.

- 1 tablespoon sweet Italian vermouth
- ¼ cup olive oil
- 1 tablespoon fresh sage leaves or *pinch dried sage*
- 1 teaspoon minced fresh oregano
  Salt and freshly ground black pepper
- 1 pound chicken or duck livers, trimmed of all fat
- 1 recipe Cipolle al Forno (see page 22)
- 2 tablespoons minced fresh chives or parsley, for garnish

1. Put vermouth, olive oil, sage, oregano, and salt and pepper to taste in a stainless steel, glass, or ceramic bowl. Add livers, toss to coat well, and let marinate, refrigerated, 12 hours or overnight.

2. Prepare a medium-hot charcoal fire. Soak 8 wooden or bamboo skewers in water to cover for 30 minutes. Thread livers on skewers. Grill quickly to brown livers well outside but keep them pink within. Transfer skewers to a serving platter and surround with Cipolle al Forno. Garnish with minced chives or parsley.

Serves 4 as a main course or 8 as a first course.

POLLO CON CAVOLO AL LIMONE
Lemon chicken with lemon cabbage

This lemon-scented chicken is first roasted in the oven, then finished by braising on a bed of shredded cabbage. The cabbage absorbs the roasting juices, the chicken becomes tender, and the finished dish far surpasses its modest ingredients. A bottle of Pinot Grigio is an excellent complement. The dish comes from The Marches.

- 1 roasting chicken (about 4 lb)
  Salt and freshly ground black pepper
- 1 lemon
- ½ cup plus 1 tablespoon unsalted butter
- ¼ cup plus 2 tablespoons lemon juice
- ¼ cup olive oil
  Grated rind of 1 lemon
- 2 pounds green cabbage, finely shredded
- ½ cup dry white wine
- 2 tablespoons white wine vinegar
- 1 teaspoon sugar

1. Preheat oven to 425° F. Season chicken inside and out with salt and pepper. Grate rind of lemon; halve lemon. Place rind and lemon in chicken cavity. Melt ¼ cup of the butter; add ¼ cup of the lemon juice and 1 tablespoon of the olive oil. Brush mixture all over chicken. Put chicken on a rack in a roasting pan breast side up; roast 25 minutes.

2. Place remaining butter and remaining oil in a Dutch oven over moderate heat; heat until butter melts. Add lemon rind and sauté

1 minute. Add cabbage and toss to coat with butter and oil. Turn up heat and add remaining lemon juice, the wine, vinegar, and sugar, and salt and pepper to taste. When mixture bubbles and sizzles, turn heat to low, cover and cook 20 minutes.

3. Remove chicken from oven and place on top of cabbage. Cover and continue cooking over moderately low heat until chicken tests done, 25 to 30 minutes. Remove chicken to cutting board. Taste cabbage and add more lemon, salt, or pepper as necessary. Carve chicken and arrange it in the center of a large warmed platter. Surround with cabbage. Pour pan juices over chicken and serve.

Serves 4.

POLLO NOVELLO ALLA CACCIATORA
Cornish hens, hunter's style

Pollo alla cacciatora turns up on Italian restaurant menus all over the United States because it can easily be made ahead and reheated. Unfortunately, it sometimes tastes as if it's been steadily reheating for months. The version below, from Tuscany, is lively and light, for the birds are first roasted and then topped with a sauce made at the last minute from pan juices, mushrooms, and tomatoes. An elegant party dish, it can also be made with split baby chickens.

> 6 *Rock Cornish game hens, split down the back and backbone removed*
> *Salt and freshly ground black pepper*
> 3 *tablespoons olive oil*
> 4 *tablespoons butter*
> 3 *cups thinly sliced mushrooms*
> 2 *shallots, minced*
> ½ *cup dry white wine*
> 1¼ *cups chicken stock*
> 3 *tablespoons brandy*
> 1 *pound tomatoes (canned or fresh), peeled, seeded, and chopped (see page 29)*
> *Parsley sprigs, for garnish*

1. Preheat oven to 350° F. Season game hens well with salt and pepper. Heat olive oil and 2 tablespoons of

the butter in a large skillet over medium-high heat. Brown hens well, in batches if necessary, transferring them to a roasting pan when they are browned. Cover pan and roast until hens are fork-tender, about 50 minutes. Transfer hens to a plate, cover with foil, and keep warm in a low oven. Pour off and reserve any juices in the roasting pan.

2. In a large skillet over medium heat, melt remaining butter. Add mushrooms and sauté until softened. With a slotted spoon remove mushrooms; set aside. Spoon off any fat accumulated on top of reserved roasting juices, then add juices to skillet. Add shallots and cook 4 minutes. Add wine and cook over moderately high heat until wine evaporates. Add stock and reduce by one half. Add brandy and carefully flame with a long match. When flames die down, add tomatoes and cook until heated through. Return mushrooms to skillet. Season to taste with salt and pepper.

3. Transfer game hens to a warmed serving platter. Spoon sauce over them. Garnish platter with parsley sprigs and serve immediately.

Serves 6.

Tender young Cornish hens prepared alla cacciatora are a pleasing variation on the usual chicken dish. Authentic Italian bread, such as the twisted baguette shown here, is always a good addition to the meal.

A DINNER TO HONOR A FINE OLD CHIANTI

Pasta con Funghi

Zucchine, Cipolle, e Carciofi Fritti

Anitra al Chianti

Spinaci con Pignoli
(see page 108)

Parmigiano Reggiano

Pesche al Vino
(see page 114)

Biscotti per il Vino

The traditional scheme of a wine dinner is to progress from white to red, from young to old, from light to heavy. The creamy mushroom sauce on the pasta suggests a fragrant, full-bodied white, such as a Pinot Grigio or a Tocai. The same wine can also accompany the small Fried Course, but switch to a fruity, medium-bodied red for the duck. The same young Chianti that you use in the marinade is a suitable choice. Save the wine of honor for the cheese course: a moist Parmigiano Reggiano, sliced thin.

PASTA CON FUNGHI
Linguine with field and wild mushrooms

Unless you collect them yourself, wild mushrooms can be expensive, but their flavor far surpasses that of the common cultivated variety. Mix wild and cultivated types to hold down the cost of this Piedmontese dish, and be sure you buy the wild mushrooms from a knowledgeable source that can positively identify them as edible. Clean mushrooms carefully with a soft toothbrush or a mushroom brush. The wild varieties in particular are usually too delicate to wash.

  4 *quarts lightly salted water*
  4 *tablespoons unsalted butter*
  1 *tablespoon olive oil*
  1 *shallot, minced*
2½ *tablespoons minced garlic*
  ½ *pound medium cultivated field mushrooms, cleaned and quartered*
  ½ *pound fresh porcini or other wild mushrooms, cleaned and halved*
  3 *tablespoons Chianti or other dry red wine*
  3 *tablespoons whipping cream*
      Salt
      Freshly ground black pepper
  ⅓ *cup minced fresh chives*
  1 *pound fresh linguine (use Pasta Gialla, page 34)*

1. In a large pot over high heat, bring the water to a boil. While water is heating melt butter and oil in a large skillet over moderately low heat. Add shallots and garlic; cook gently 3 minutes. Add mushrooms, raise heat to high, and cook briskly 3 minutes. Add wine and let evaporate over high heat. Add cream and reduce slightly. Remove from heat; add salt and black pepper to taste. Gently stir in half of the minced chives.

2. Add pasta to rapidly boiling water and cook until just done. Drain well in a colander and transfer to a warm serving bowl. Add sauce and toss well. Garnish with remaining minced chives and serve hot.

Serves 4.

In front are pasta and the Fried Course. Braised duck, spinach, and the cheese flank the honored Chianti. Dessert is marinated peaches with wine rusks.

ZUCCHINE, CIPOLLE, E CARCIOFI FRITTI
The Fried Course: zucchini, onions, and artichokes

Florentine cooks are expert at deep-frying; in fact, the traditional Florentine meal includes a separate fried course. The batter and vegetables are prepared ahead, leaving only the whipping of egg whites and the frying for the last minute. Use a thermometer to keep oil temperature constant.

    2 cups cake flour
    1 teaspoon coarse salt
    ¼ cup olive oil
    3 eggs, separated
    1⅓ cups cold water
    3 tablespoons dry red wine
    1 teaspoon freshly ground
       black pepper
    2 medium zucchini
    4 small onions, about 2 inches
       in diameter
    4 small artichokes, no larger
       than 1½ inches in diameter
       Corn or peanut oil, for
       deep-frying
       Gremolata (see page 77)

1. In a large bowl stir flour and salt together. In a small bowl whisk together olive oil and egg yolks. Slowly add oil-egg mixture to flour. Whisk in water, wine, and pepper. Set aside at room temperature for 2 hours.

2. Trim ends of zucchini. Cut zucchini in half lengthwise, then cut each half crosswise into thirds. Peel onions and halve them. When you are ready to cook, prepare artichoke hearts according to the directions on page 16. Halve them (top to bottom) and remove any fuzzy inner choke.

3. Heat at least 4 inches of oil in a large kettle or deep fryer to 375° F. While oil is heating, whip egg whites with a pinch of salt until stiff but not dry. Fold into batter. Dip vegetables, a few at a time, in batter; fry until golden brown. As they brown, remove with a slotted spoon to paper towels to drain, then keep warm in low oven. When all are fried, arrange on a warm serving platter or on individual plates; garnish with Gremolata.

Serves 4.

ANITRA AL CHIANTI
Duck braised in young Chianti

The fruitiness of a young Chianti flatters the sweet flavor of duck. For this Tuscan dish, marinate the duck overnight in Chianti, then braise it slowly in the same wine with herbs and aromatic vegetables. The finished bird will be fork-tender, the resultant sauce rich and mellow.

    2 ducks (about 4 lb each), pref-
       erably fresh
    2 carrots, coarsely chopped
    2 large onions, peeled and
       cut into eighths
    1 celery stalk, coarsely chopped
    1 bay leaf
    1 sprig fresh thyme or
       1 teaspoon ground thyme
    6 garlic cloves, unpeeled
    1 bottle (750 ml) young Chianti
    ¼ cup flour
    2 to 2½ cups duck or chicken
       stock

1. Wash ducks inside and out and dry thoroughly with paper towels. Remove any visible fat (reserve for another use). Cut ducks into quarters. Put duck into a ceramic, stainless steel, or glass bowl and add carrots, onion, celery, bay leaf, and thyme. Smash garlic lightly with the side of a knife and add to bowl along with wine. Cover bowl with plastic wrap and let marinate at room temperature for about 12 hours (refrigerate in very hot weather). Remove duck pieces from marinade and pat dry. Strain marinade and reserve both strained wine and vegetables.

2. Heat a large, heavy skillet over moderately high heat. Add duck pieces and brown well on all sides. The duck will render considerable fat. Pour fat off as it accumulates; save it for browning potatoes or cooking omelets. When duck is well browned, transfer it to a plate and pour off all but 2 tablespoons fat.

3. Preheat oven to 350° F. Add marinade vegetables to fat in skillet and sauté over moderate heat until somewhat tender, about 5 minutes. Add flour and sauté an additional 3 minutes, stirring. Transfer vegetables to a baking dish just large enough to hold the duck in 1 layer and arrange duck pieces on top. Add reserved wine and about 2 cups stock. The liquid should come about halfway up the sides of the duck. Cover with foil and braise ducks in oven until fork-tender and richly colored, about 1½ hours. Check occasionally and add more liquid if necessary to maintain the same level.

4. When duck is done, transfer pieces to a serving platter and keep warm. Strain the sauce through a sieve, let settle briefly, then carefully remove as much fat as possible with a spoon. Put the degreased sauce in a saucepan and reduce over high heat to 1¼ cups. Pour sauce over duck and serve immediately.

Serves 4.

BISCOTTI PER IL VINO
Wine rusks

Almost every Italian bakery sells several varieties of dry *biscotti*, twice-baked *(bis cotto)* cookies that are meant to be dunked in either coffee or wine. To bring your dinner to an authentic Tuscan end, serve these along with the Pesche al Vino (see page 114) and encourage guests to soften the rusks in the wine syrup. They keep for weeks in an airtight container; offer them with afternoon tea or coffee or with a late-night glass of sweet wine. Note that the dough must chill at least 1 night.

    ¼ cup dried currants
    2 tablespoons Marsala
    ½ pound unsalted butter,
       softened
    2 cups sugar
    4 eggs
    1 teaspoon vanilla extract
    1 tablespoon anise-flavored
       apéritif

4 cups flour
1 teaspoon baking powder
1 teaspoon baking soda
½ teaspoon salt
2 teaspoons grated lemon rind
1 teaspoon aniseed
½ cup half-and-half
1 cup coarsely chopped toasted walnuts
1 cup coarsely chopped toasted hazelnuts

1. Put currants in a bowl with Marsala; soak for 20 minutes.

2. Cream butter; add sugar gradually and beat until light. Add eggs one at a time, beating until light and fluffy. Add vanilla, apéritif, and currants with their soaking liquid.

3. Sift together flour, baking powder, baking soda, and salt. Stir in lemon rind and aniseed. Add to creamed mixture alternately with half-and-half. Stir in walnuts and hazelnuts by hand. Cover and chill dough for at least 2 hours or overnight.

4. Divide dough into quarters and place each quarter on a length of waxed paper. Form into a roll about 15 inches long and 1½ inches thick. Wrap in waxed paper, then in foil. Chill overnight (dough can be frozen at this point for up to 1 month; bring frozen dough to refrigerator temperature before proceeding).

5. Preheat oven to 350° F. Unwrap rolls and place them on ungreased baking sheets. Bake until very lightly browned, about 20 to 25 minutes. Carefully transfer rolls to a cutting board and cut on a 45° angle into slices about ½ inch thick. Place slices cut side up on the baking sheets and return to oven. Bake until golden, about 8 to 12 minutes. Cool rusks thoroughly on racks. Store in airtight containers.

Makes about 4 dozen rusks.

GAMBE D'ANITRA ALLA GRIGLIA
Grilled duck legs with garlic and balsamic vinegar

A purée of garlic stuffed under the skin perfumes these grilled duck legs, with balsamic vinegar adding its sweet-tart flavor. Roasting the legs first releases most of the fat; they can then be quickly finished on the grill. Serve the duck legs with Bruschetta (see page 13) and an assortment of grilled vegetables, or offer a salad of shredded romaine dressed with olive oil, balsamic vinegar, and Parmesan. The recipe comes from the town of Maremma, near Grosseto in Tuscany.

2 tablespoons unsalted butter
½ cup olive oil
3 heads garlic, cloves separated and peeled but left whole
6 fresh oregano sprigs
  Salt and freshly ground black pepper
4 tablespoons dry white wine
12 duck legs and thighs, in one piece
½ cup balsamic vinegar
10 tablespoons olive oil

1. In a medium skillet over moderate heat, melt butter with oil. Add garlic, oregano, and salt and pepper to taste. Cook gently 30 minutes. Garlic cloves should be very soft. Add wine, reduce by half over high heat, then remove skillet from heat. Remove oregano sprigs. Purée the garlic in a food processor or blender.

2. Using 1½ teaspoons garlic purée per duck piece, spread purée between the skin and the flesh. Combine vinegar, olive oil, and any remaining purée. Put duck in a stainless steel, enamel, or glass bowl or baking dish and cover with vinegar mixture. Marinate 2 hours at room temperature (or in refrigerator if weather is warm).

3. Preheat oven to 350° F. Prepare a medium-hot charcoal fire. Remove duck from marinade and place on a rack in a roasting pan. Roast 30 minutes in preheated oven, basting with marinade twice. Finish cooking duck on the grill to crisp the skin.

Serves 6 to 8.

POLLO ALLA DIAVOLA
Deviled chicken

For this Roman dish, brush flattened broiler halves with a peppery lemon and mustard mixture, then broil slowly and baste until the skin crisps and browns. The result is a devilishly good *diavola*, to serve with wilted greens and a basket of crunchy toast topped with fennel seed and pepper.

2 broiling chickens (about 3 lb each)
1 shallot, minced
1 teaspoon grated lemon rind
2 teaspoons lemon juice
½ teaspoon hot red-pepper flakes
2 tablespoons olive oil
1 tablespoon red wine vinegar
1 tablespoon Dijon-style mustard
¼ cup dry white wine
¼ cup unsalted butter, melted
1 recipe Pane per la Zuppa (see page 49)

1. Halve the chickens lengthwise and remove any fatty deposits. Place halves between sheets of waxed paper or parchment paper. Using the flat side of a large cleaver or a mallet, pound the chickens flat. (It doesn't matter if the bones crack.)

2. Whisk together shallot, lemon rind, lemon juice, red-pepper flakes, olive oil, vinegar, and mustard. Combine wine and butter in a small bowl.

3. Preheat broiler. Coat chickens well with olive oil mixture and place on a broiler rack, skin side down. Position rack at least 6 inches from heat and broil about 12 minutes, basting occasionally with wine-butter mixture. Turn chicken and continue broiling and basting for about 10 minutes more. When chicken is done, remove to a heated platter and pour any leftover olive oil mixture over it. Serve immediately with a basket of Pane per la Zuppa.

Serves 6.

Pollo alla Griglia con Salsa d'Aglio makes a perfect patio meal. The chicken, marinated in garlic, olive oil, rosemary, and wine, cooks on the grill while the accompanying potato slices bake. Serve with garlic mayonnaise and a lightly chilled Grignolino. A salad of sliced tomatoes, mozzarella, and basil can open the meal.

POLLO TOSCANO CON PEPERONI E CARCIOFI
Tuscan chicken with peppers and artichokes

American southerners aren't the only cooks who use cornmeal in frying. The practice is popular in Tuscany, too. Tuscan cooks coat chicken with cornmeal, then brown it quickly, braise it in wine, and smother it with sweet peppers and artichokes. The multicolored dish needs no garnish or accompaniment other than a bottle of hearty red wine.

- ¾ cup flour
- ¼ cup cornmeal
- 1 teaspoon dried oregano
- 1 teaspoon dried basil
- 1 teaspoon salt
- 14 chicken legs
- 4 tablespoons olive oil
- 4 tablespoons butter
- 1 cup chopped onion
- 3 tablespoons minced garlic
- ¾ cup dry white wine
- 2 cups chicken stock
- ¼ cup cream
- ½ cup fresh basil leaves, roughly torn

Pepper and Artichoke Garnish

- 6 baby artichokes
- 1 lemon, halved
- ⅓ cup olive oil
- 1 tablespoon minced garlic
- 1 cup thinly sliced green bell pepper
- 1 cup thinly sliced yellow bell pepper
- 1 cup thinly sliced red bell pepper
- 4 sprigs fresh oregano, leaves only
  Coarse salt

1. Combine flour, cornmeal, oregano, basil, and salt. Dredge chicken legs in mixture, shaking off excess. In a large skillet over moderate heat, melt oil and butter. Add legs and brown, in batches if necessary. Transfer legs to a plate as they finish browning.

2. Add onion and garlic to the skillet and sauté gently 10 to 12 minutes. Add wine, stock, and browned chicken legs (if necessary, transfer half the mixture and half the legs to another skillet). Cover and simmer gently 30 minutes.

3. Test chicken legs for doneness. When juices run clear, transfer chicken legs to a warmed serving platter and keep warm. Strain the chicken liquid through a fine sieve into a clean skillet. Add cream and reduce by one third. Add Pepper and Artichoke Garnish. Taste and adjust seasoning as necessary. Add basil leaves and chicken. Turn to coat chicken with sauce, then transfer to serving dish.

Serves 6.

Pepper and Artichoke Garnish

1. Peel away tough, dark green outer leaves of artichokes until you reach the pale green heart. Trim stem ends. Cut about ½ inch off the tip with a sharp knife. Put hearts in a bowl of water acidulated with the juice of half a lemon (to prevent browning). Bring a medium pot of salted water to a boil over high heat. Add juice and pulp of remaining half lemon. Drain artichoke hearts and add them to boiling water. Cook until just tender when pierced with the tip of a knife. Drain well and dry. (Preparation of baby artichoke hearts is illustrated on page 16.)

2. Heat olive oil in a skillet over moderately low heat. Add garlic and sauté 1 minute. Add peppers and oregano, raise heat to medium, and cook, covered, for 15 minutes. Taste and add salt if necessary. Add artichokes, stir to blend, and cook just until they are hot.

POLLO ALLA GRIGLIA CON SALSA D'AGLIO
Grilled chicken with garlic sauce

Spread out the red-and-white cloth, open some cool Grignolino, and serve this casual Tuscan dinner for patio parties. The creamy garlic mayonnaise can be slathered on chicken hot off the grill or on herbed, oven-baked potatoes. Leftover mayonnaise is great on tomato salads, cold chicken, or an egg salad sandwich.

- ½ cup olive oil
- 2 tablespoons minced garlic
- 3 sprigs fresh rosemary
- ¼ cup dry white wine
  Salt and freshly ground black pepper
- 1 roasting chicken (about 4 lb), in 8 pieces
- 3 baking potatoes
- 2 tablespoons minced shallots
- ¼ cup unsalted butter, melted
- 1 tablespoon lemon juice
- 4 sprigs fresh thyme

Garlic Sauce

- 4 tablespoons olive oil
- 2 tablespoons peanut oil
- 1 egg yolk
  Juice of ½ lemon
- 1½ teaspoons minced garlic
- 2 tablespoons cream
- 1 tablespoon freshly grated Parmesan
  Salt and freshly ground black pepper

1. To marinate the chicken: Heat olive oil in a saucepan over moderately low heat. Add garlic and sauté gently 5 minutes; do not let garlic brown. Remove from heat and add rosemary and wine. Cool slightly. Salt and pepper chicken pieces and put them in a stainless steel, glass, or ceramic bowl or baking dish. Cover with wine mixture and marinate, refrigerated, 3 to 12 hours.

2. About 30 minutes before serving, prepare potatoes as follows: If potatoes are russets, peel them; there's no need to peel thin-skinned potatoes. Slice them into rounds ¼ inch thick and arrange them in a single layer on a large baking sheet. Combine shallots, butter, and lemon juice and pour over the potatoes. Arrange thyme sprigs on top.

3. Prepare a medium-hot charcoal fire. Preheat oven to 450° F. Remove chicken from marinade and place on grill. Grill chicken, turning occasionally and basting with marinade, until it is done to your liking, about 20 to 25 minutes. Fifteen minutes (approximately) before chicken is done, put potatoes in oven. Roast 10 to 15 minutes, turning them over as they brown. When potatoes are done, season them with salt and pepper, turn off the oven, and leave them in the oven with the door ajar until the chicken is ready. Serve chicken and potatoes family-style with Garlic Sauce on the side.

Serves 3 to 4.

Garlic Sauce Combine the two oils and set aside. Put egg yolk, lemon juice, and garlic in workbowl of food processor fitted with steel blade or in blender. Process until yolk is pale yellow. With the machine running, slowly add the oil through the feed tube to make a mayonnaise, then slowly add the cream. When sauce is thick, transfer it to a bowl and stir in Parmesan by hand. Season to taste with salt and pepper. If you are not going to use the sauce immediately, it can be stored, covered, in the refrigerator. Before serving it, be sure to bring it to room temperature.

Vegetables shine in Italian salads and side dishes. Salad dressings are often very simple, showcasing the fine vinegars and olive oils for which Italy is renowned.

Salads & Vegetables

Italian salads and vegetable dishes generally reflect the seasons. In this chapter you'll find a salad based on the tender, young vegetables of spring (see Una Piccola Insalata di Primavera, page 100), one that uses summer's wealth of tomatoes and zucchini (see Insalata dell' Estate, page 101), and a winter salad of beets and turnips (see Insalata dell' Inverno, page 102). There is a recipe for spring's asparagus and new onions (see Asparagi di Primavera, page 106), one for June's peas (see Piselli al Prosciutto, page 108), and one for a summer tomato casserole (see Pomodori dell' Estate, page 109). The chapter also includes a menu for a Cold Supper (see page 104).

Tuscan cooks take advantage of day-old bread to make Panzanella, a lively summer salad that can be a one-dish lunch.

SALADS

The most common Italian salad is made of raw greens alone, lightly dressed with olive oil and vinegar. But Italians also love to make salads out of tender, young seasonal vegetables. In spring they combine carrots and radishes in a light mustard dressing or serve the first fava beans and asparagus with oil and lemon. In summer, squash and tomatoes are bathed in an herb marinade. Autumn brings eggplant, fried and layered with garlic and vinegar. Winter salads of beets and their greens are often supplemented with turnips and dressed with anchovy, lemon, and oil.

The broad-minded cook can find salad makings in every season's harvest. Italian cooks do, and you'll find a few of their best ideas in the collection that follows.

VINAIGRETTE

The simplest and possibly the best vinaigrette is made at the table. Offer a cruet of light virgin olive oil, a cruet of fine red wine vinegar, a dish of coarse salt, and a pepper mill and let guests dress their own salad to taste.

Vinaigrettes may be made several hours ahead. They may be stored, covered, in the refrigerator for up to one week with only slight loss of flavor. Bring to room temperature, taste, and reseason before reusing.

The basic vinaigrette, below, is excellent for salads made with heartier greens, such as romaine, dandelion greens, and chicory.

> *Juice of 1 lemon*
> 4 *tablespoons red wine vinegar*
> *Coarse salt to taste*
> ¾ *cup olive oil*
> 1 *teaspoon freshly ground black pepper*

In a small bowl, combine lemon, vinegar, and salt. Stir to dissolve salt. Whisk in olive oil. Let sit 10 minutes. Add pepper, taste, and add more salt if needed.

Makes about 1 cup.

Balsamic Vinaigrette Substitute balsamic vinegar for the red wine vinegar.

Lemon Vinaigrette Substitute lemon juice for the red wine vinegar. This is an excellent vinaigrette for salads with a fruit or fish component.

Anchovy Vinaigrette

This lively dressing is particularly good on a salad served before a rustic main course, such as pizza or calzone.

- 3 anchovy fillets, minced
- 4 tablespoons red wine vinegar
  Juice of 1 lemon
- ¾ cup olive oil
- 2 tablespoons freshly grated Parmesan
- 1 teaspoon freshly ground black pepper

In a small bowl, whisk together anchovy, vinegar, and lemon juice. Whisk in olive oil, then stir in Parmesan and pepper.

Makes about 1 cup.

PANZANELLA
Tuscan bread salad

This colorful salad owes a debt to some resourceful cook who couldn't bear to throw away the day-old bread. Many of Florence's *trattorie* have this cool salad on the menu all summer. Note that the cubed bread must sit out overnight and the vegetables must marinate at least 2 hours.

- ½ loaf day-old dense country-style bread
- 3 medium tomatoes, peeled, seeded, and chopped
- 1 cucumber, peeled, seeded, and diced
- 1 red bell pepper, seeded and diced

- 1 small red onion, in paper-thin rings
- ¼ cup diced giardiniera (Italian pickles)
- 3 tablespoons drained small capers
- ½ cup minced parsley
- ¼ cup red wine vinegar
- ¼ cup Dijon mustard
- 1 ounce anchovy fillets, minced (optional)
- 2 teaspoons minced fresh oregano
- 1 cup olive oil
  Salt and freshly ground black pepper
  Additional red onion slices, for garnish
  Imported unpitted black olives, for garnish (optional)
  Additional anchovy fillets, for garnish (optional)
- 3 tablespoons minced parsley, for garnish

1. Cut bread into 1-inch cubes. Spread cubes out on a tray and let sit overnight to harden.

2. Combine tomatoes, cucumber, red pepper, onion, pickles, capers, and parsley in a large nonreactive bowl; mix gently but well. Set aside.

3. In a small bowl, combine vinegar, mustard, minced anchovies (if used), and oregano. Whisk in olive oil. Add salt and pepper to taste. Pour over mixed vegetables, stir to blend, and let sit at room temperature at least 2 hours or overnight, covered, in a cool place.

4. About 20 minutes before serving, combine 2 cups of the bread cubes with the marinated vegetables. Taste and adjust salt and pepper as needed. Add additional red onion slices, and olives, if used. Just before serving, stir in remaining bread cubes, pile salad onto a serving platter and top with anchovy fillets (if used) and parsley.

Serves 4 generously.

Basics

OLIVE OIL

Some of the world's best olive oil comes from Italy. Although some northern dishes are made with butter, it is olive oil that gives most Italian cooking its characteristic flavor.

The flavor of the oil varies according to the type of olives it is pressed from, the region where the olives are grown, and the method of pressing. The best oils have a clean, fruity aroma, a full but not heavy body, and a fruity or peppery flavor.

Olive oils are categorized according to their acidity and the procedure used to make them. To merit one of the top four categories, the oil must be pressed from olives that have not been subjected to chemical treatments of any kind.

Extravirgin olive oil contains no more than 1 percent oleic acid.

Superfine virgin olive oil contains no more than 1½ percent oleic acid.

Fine virgin olive oil contains no more than 3 percent oleic acid.

Virgin olive oil contains no more than 4 percent oleic acid.

Olive oil that contains more than 4 percent oleic acid is considered unfit for human consumption. Many large olive oil manufacturers treat such oil with chemical solvents to reduce the acid below 4 percent, then add some virgin olive oil to improve the flavor. The result may be called pure olive oil or *olio d'oliva*.

Heat changes the character of an olive oil. For frying or sautéing, it makes little sense to use an expensive extravirgin oil, whose character would change in the process. Use a good-tasting affordable olive oil and save your best oils for uncooked dishes or for drizzling on cooked dishes at the end of the cooking time.

Store all olive oils in a cool, dark place—they go rancid when exposed to heat and light. Use within a year.

FAGIOLI BIANCHI CON PEPERONATA
White bean salad with peppers

White beans and red peppers are a happy match that's found all over Italy—as a picnic salad, as an antipasto, or as a side dish to cold roast lamb. Dress them while they're warm so that they absorb the flavors of lemon, oil, and onion. Note that beans must soak for an hour.

2 cups dried white beans
½ white onion, stuck with 2 cloves
1 bay leaf
1 large sprig thyme
2 sprigs parsley
2 teaspoons salt
⅓ cup olive oil
½ cup peeled, seeded, and diced tomatoes (see page 29)
2 green onions, minced
2 sun-dried tomatoes (from jar), slivered
2 tablespoons oil from sun-dried tomatoes
2 tablespoons lemon juice
1 tablespoon white wine vinegar
1 recipe Peperonata (see page 13)
Lettuce leaves (optional)
4 thick slices of Pane Toscano (see page 48), brushed well with olive oil and grilled or toasted

1. Cover beans with cold water and soak 1 hour. Drain; place beans in a large kettle. Add onion, bay leaf, thyme, parsley, and salt. Cover with water; bring to a boil. Reduce heat; simmer until beans are just tender, about 45 minutes. Drain; discard onion, bay leaf, thyme, and parsley.

2. Cool beans slightly; place in a stainless steel, glass, or ceramic bowl. Add olive oil, tomatoes, green onions, sun-dried tomatoes and their oil, lemon juice, and vinegar. Cool to room temperature; taste and add salt if needed.

3. Stir in Peperonata, then serve salad as is or atop lettuce leaves. Accompany with warm grilled bread.

Serves 4.

UNA PICCOLA INSALATA DI PRIMAVERA
A little salad of spring vegetables

In early spring the Bologna markets are filled with tiny golden carrots and sweet young radishes, red and white. Grated and tossed with a mustard dressing, they make a light and refreshing spring salad to precede Arrosto di Maiale con Rosmarino (see page 84) or a baked Easter ham.

4 to 6 small carrots
12 radishes
2 heads romaine
1 bunch arugula or radish sprouts (optional)
2 teaspoons Dijon mustard
¼ cup red wine vinegar
Grated rind of ½ lemon
½ cup full-flavored olive oil
Salt and freshly ground black pepper
Lemon juice
12 slices Bruschetta (see page 13)
2 tablespoons coarsely grated Parmesan (optional)

1. Wash and scrub carrots and radishes. Grate them coarsely by hand or in the food processor. Wash and dry romaine; remove outer leaves and reserve for another use. Wrap hearts in damp paper towels and refrigerate until ready to use. If you are using arugula, wash and dry it; wrap in damp paper towels and refrigerate.

2. In a medium bowl whisk together mustard and vinegar. Add lemon rind and slowly whisk in olive oil. Add salt, pepper, and lemon juice (up to 1 tablespoon) to taste. Add carrots and radishes to bowl and toss to coat with dressing. Marinate at room temperature for about 20 minutes.

3. To serve, arrange romaine hearts, Bruschetta, and arugula (if used) on individual plates. Top with vegetables, spooning some of vegetables and dressing over bread rounds. Garnish, if desired, with Parmesan.

Serves 4.

INSALATA CAPRICCIOSA
Classic "capricious" salad

This classic is a salad for summer, when the tomatoes and basil are at their best. Use only sweet, vine-ripened tomatoes, and visit a cheese merchant for the finest whole-milk mozzarella. A hot loaf of crusty Pane Toscano (see page 48) should be on the table, too.

8 ounces fresh whole-milk mozzarella or imported buffalo-milk mozzarella, at room temperature
4 tomatoes, at room temperature, cored and thinly sliced
½ cup extravirgin olive oil
Juice of 1½ large or 2 small lemons
¼ cup shredded fresh basil leaves
Coarse salt and freshly ground black pepper
Additional basil sprigs, for garnish

1. Slice cheese into rounds about ⅛ inch thick. On a large serving platter or on individual salad plates, arrange alternate slices of cheese and tomato in a concentric pattern.

2. In a small bowl combine olive oil, lemon juice, and basil. Whisk well. Spoon dressing over salad. Season with salt and pepper. Garnish with basil sprigs and serve immediately.

Serves 4 as a first course.

INSALATA MISTA
Wild and gathered greens

The typical Italian green salad is simply the freshest seasonal greens in a light oil-and-vinegar dressing. But the range of salad greens used in Italy astounds many American visitors. who may be familiar with only a couple of the varieties. Fortunately, more big-city markets are stocking an assortment of greens and herbs. Look for a market that takes care of its greens, then make your salad with whatever is freshest and dress it lightly with a vinaigrette. When you toss the salad, use wooden utensils if possible; metal utensils bruise the leaves, and the heat of one's hands can wilt this delicate salad.

Mixed greens: Choose from hearts of romaine, butter lettuce, red-leaf lettuce, limestone lettuce, Belgian endive, arugula, radicchio, purple kale, dandelion greens, tender radish tops, young sorrel leaves, fresh oregano, whole small basil leaves, thyme flowers, chive flowers
Vinaigrette (see pages 98–99)

1. Carefully wash greens; dry thoroughly. Do not break up or chop them. Wrap in damp paper towels; refrigerate until serving time. Chill salad plates and bowl slightly.

2. To serve, toss greens with vinaigrette. Divide among salad plates or serve from the bowl. Offer a pepper mill at the table.

INSALATA DELL' ESTATE
Summer salad of zucchini and tomatoes

Italian cooks turn squash and tomatoes into a sprightly summer salad by adding oil, vinegar, and lots of fresh herbs. Mint marks this version as a Roman dish; in Rome, diners spoon it into the hollows of hard, crusty rolls.

½ pound each *small, firm green zucchini and yellow crookneck squash*
2 tablespoons *white wine vinegar*
½ cup *olive oil*
3 tablespoons *minced parsley*
1 tablespoon each *minced fresh chives and mint*
4 *tomatoes, peeled, seeded, and diced*
1 head each *butter and red-leaf lettuce*
⅓ cup *minced prosciutto*
Salt
1 teaspoon *freshly ground black pepper*
Additional mint leaves, for garnish

1. Grate zucchini and squash coarsely. In a large bowl whisk together vinegar, oil, parsley, chives, and mint. Add zucchini, squash, and tomatoes; stir gently and set aside.

2. Wash and dry lettuces; tear into bite-sized pieces. Arrange on a large serving platter. Just before serving, mix prosciutto into vegetables. Salt to taste; add pepper. Pile vegetables onto platter; garnish with mint leaves.

Serves 4.

Use the freshest young greens that you can find for an Insalata Mista—shown here are endive, butter lettuce, dandelion, purple kale, arugula, and romaine, garnished with chive blossoms—and dress it simply with fine olive oil and vinegar.

Beets with their greens and young turnips make a distinctive winter salad. Serve Insalata dell' Inverno before Arrosto di Maiale con Rosmarino (see page 84), a Sicilian-style pork roast with rosemary.

INSALATA DELL' INVERNO
Winter salad of beets and turnips

Most Italians are as fond of the beet greens and stems as they are of the sweet round beets. The greens are blanched, dressed, and served alone as a salad; or, as here, they're mixed with beets and turnips for a heartier first course. Note that beets must bake for 1½ hours.

> 3 or 4 medium *beets with greens attached*
> 7 or 8 small *turnips*
> 2 tablespoons each *lemon juice and red wine vinegar*
> 1 tablespoon *Dijon mustard*
> ½ tablespoon *anchovy paste*
> ½ cup plus 2 tablespoons *olive oil*
> 3 tablespoons *freshly grated Parmesan*
> *Salt and freshly ground black pepper*
> ½ head each *green-leaf and romaine lettuce, washed and dried*
> 2 tablespoons *minced parsley*

1. Preheat oven to 375° F. Remove beet greens and stems and set aside. Wash beets and put them in an ovenproof bowl or baking dish. Add water to come halfway up the sides of the beets, then cover tightly with a lid or aluminum foil and bake until beets can be easily pierced with a knife, about 1½ hours. Remove from oven and let cool. While beets are still warm, peel them and slice into rounds, then into thin matchsticks.

2. Wash beet stems and greens, then separate stems from greens. Bring a large pot of salted water to a boil and blanch greens 30 seconds. Transfer greens with a slotted spoon to a bowl of ice water. Drain and pat thoroughly dry. Boil stems 1 minute in same water; transfer to ice water and, when cool, drain and dry them. Chop both beet greens and stems coarsely.

3. In a large bowl, combine lemon juice, vinegar, mustard, and anchovy paste. Whisk in the ½ cup olive oil. Stir in 1 tablespoon of the Parmesan. Add beet greens and stems and marinate 15 minutes.

4. Bring another large pot of salted water to a boil. Wash turnips, then boil under tender. Very small turnips may take only 10 minutes, larger turnips up to 45 minutes. Drain and dry. While still warm, peel turnips, slice into rounds, then into thin matchsticks. Very small turnips may be left whole or halved.

5. Add beets, turnips, and remaining 2 tablespoons oil to marinating beet greens; let marinate 20 minutes. Add salt and pepper to taste. Line a serving platter with lettuce and romaine leaves. Top with salad. Combine remaining Parmesan and the parsley and sprinkle over salad.

Serves 4.

INSALATA DI FAVE
Fresh fava bean salad

Meaty fava beans are an Italian favorite from north to south: in soups and stews, as a hot first course with olive oil and salt, or as a cool spring salad. Sicilian cooks often add a pinch of hot red-pepper flakes to their beans. To make a lunch or a more substantial first course, they might serve the salad on a large platter surrounded with tomatoes, sliced prosciutto, hard-cooked eggs, and *pecorino* cheese.

- 2 *pounds fresh unshelled fava beans*
- 2 *tablespoons lemon juice*
- 1 *tablespoon white wine vinegar*
  Coarse salt
  Freshly ground black pepper
  Large pinch hot red-pepper flakes
- ½ *cup olive oil*
- ½ *cup finely minced red onion*
- 8 *tender butter-lettuce cups*
- 2 *tablespoons minced fresh chives*
- 2 *tablespoons coarsely chopped parsley*

1. Bring a large pot of water to a boil. Shell beans, add to boiling water, and boil for 2 minutes. Drain, refresh under cold running water, and pat dry.

2. In a small bowl, combine lemon juice and vinegar; add salt, black pepper, and red-pepper flakes to taste. Stir and set aside for 5 minutes to dissolve salt. Whisk in olive oil.

3. Combine beans and dressing in a serving bowl. Add onion and mix well. Set aside to marinate at least 30 minutes or up to 8 hours in a cool place. Divide lettuce cups among four salad plates. Spoon beans into lettuce cups. Garnish with chives and parsley.

Serves 4.

INSALATA DI PATATE CON CIPOLLE
Roman potato and onion salad

Dress potatoes while they're still warm and they will absorb the maximum flavor. Serve at room temperature, at picnics or patio meals, with anything from cold sliced Italian sausages to American hamburgers.

- 3 *tablespoons white wine vinegar*
- 1 *tablespoon lemon juice*
  Grated rind of 1 lemon
- 2 *tablespoons finely minced fresh oregano*
- 2 *tablespoons drained small capers*
- 1 *tablespoon coarse salt*
- 1½ *teaspoons freshly ground black pepper*
- ¾ *cup extravirgin olive oil*
- 2 *large white onions, sliced in ¼-inch rounds*
- 1½ *pounds small red potatoes*
- 3 *tablespoons minced parsley mixed with ½ tablespooon grated lemon rind, for garnish*

1. In a large bowl, combine vinegar, lemon juice, lemon rind, oregano, capers, salt, and pepper. Whisk in olive oil. Add onion slices and mix thoroughly.

2. Bring a large pot of salted water to a boil. Add potatoes and boil until barely tender. Drain, and when cool enough to handle, slice potatoes ¼ inch thick. Immediately add potatoes to dressing and toss with hands to coat well. Cool to room temperature, then taste and adjust seasoning. Garnish with minced parsley and lemon rind.

Serves 4.

INSALATA DI FINOCCHI E CARCIOFI
Fennel and artichoke salad

The first spring artichokes are a delicious partner to the last of the fennel. Marinated in oil and lemon, then served with toasts and Parmesan, the pair flatter each other and harmonize with almost any main course: Grilled fish, roast lamb, or chicken are all fine choices.

- 1 *large or 2 small fennel bulbs*
- 3 *lemons*
- ¾ *cup olive oil*
  Coarse salt and freshly ground black pepper
- 4 *small artichokes, about 2 to 3 inches in diameter*
- 12 *slices Bruschetta (see page 13)*
- 4 *ounces Parmesan, in long, thin slabs*
  Additional olive oil

1. Wash fennel bulbs and remove any tough outer stalks (see page 80). Halve and core them, and slice thinly lengthwise. Put fennel slices in a stainless steel, glass, or ceramic bowl. Add juice of 2 lemons, the olive oil, and salt and pepper to taste. Toss to blend and set aside to marinate.

2. Remove dark green outer leaves of artichokes; cut off the top third of the artichokes with a serrated knife. Rub all cut surfaces with lemon. Cook in boiling salted water until just tender, about 12 to 15 minutes. Drain and refresh under cold running water, then drain thoroughly and pat dry. Cut artichokes in half. Add to fennel in bowl and stir to coat with oil. Marinate an additional 30 to 45 minutes. Taste and add more salt or lemon if necessary.

3. To serve, spoon a little of the marinade onto individual salad plates. Arrange fennel atop marinade. Surround with slices of Bruschetta. Top bread with artichoke hearts. Place Parmesan slices between bread slices and drizzle salad with a little additional olive oil. Serve immediately and pass the pepper mill.

Serves 4.

A COLD SUPPER

Panzanella (see page 99)

Bistecca con Salsa Cruda

Funghi alla Griglia

Granita di Melone

On a balmy summer evening, tempt guests with a cold meal of Tuscan specialties. The Florentines know how to beat the heat: with a cool, vinegar-laced salad of bread and vegetables; a platter of their famous grilled beef, sliced and served cold; and a bowl of marinated mushrooms. Granita di Melone makes a fitting dessert. Do as the Florentines do and wash it down with a fresh, young Chianti that's been chilled about 20 minutes before serving. Apart from toasting the sandwich bread, the entire meal can be made well in advance.

BISTECCA CON SALSA CRUDA
Skirt steak with fresh tomato sauce

Steak sandwiches don't get any better than this Florentine version, made with marinated and grilled skirt steak, grilled bread, and a fresh (uncooked) tomato and herb sauce. A mushroom or two from the accompanying Funghi alla Griglia would make a fine addition to each sandwich. Note that the steak needs to marinate overnight and to cool after it is cooked.

- ½ bottle (375 ml) young Chianti
- 3 cloves minced garlic
- 2 tablespoons balsamic vinegar
- 1 tablespoon freshly ground black pepper
- 2 large sprigs fresh rosemary
- ½ red onion, minced
- 2 pounds skirt steak, lightly pounded
- 8 large slices Pane Toscano (see page 48), about ⅓ inch thick
  Olive oil
- 1 recipe Sugo di Pomodori Freschi (see page 36)

1. In a large bowl combine wine, garlic, vinegar, pepper, rosemary, and onion. Add meat, cover bowl with plastic wrap, refrigerate, and marinate overnight.

2. Prepare a medium-hot charcoal fire. Bring meat to room temperature. When coals have burned down to a gray ash, sear meat quickly on both sides, basting with marinade. It should be browned outside but still pink within. Set aside and let rest 10 minutes before carving.

3. Put marinade in a small saucepan and bring to a boil over high heat. Reduce to ½ cup. Remove rosemary sprigs; reserve marinade.

4. Carve meat into long thin strips across the grain. Moisten with ¼ cup of the reduced marinade. Set aside at room temperature for 1 hour or refrigerate for several hours, but bring to room temperature before serving.

5. Preheat oven to 375° F. Brush bread slices lightly with olive oil and with remaining marinade. Toast on a baking sheet until lightly colored, about 5 to 8 minutes. Pile toasts on a platter. Pile sliced steak on another platter and spoon the tomato sauce over it. Serve while toasts are warm.

Serves 4.

FUNGHI ALLA GRIGLIA
Grilled and marinated mushrooms

Mushrooms are like sponges: They readily absorb liquids, and if that liquid is a tangy marinade, it's all to the good. In the recipe below, the mushrooms are marinated briefly, then grilled in a foil pan over coals. After grilling, they're returned to the marinade to cool and reabsorb its flavors. Serve the mushrooms at room temperature.

- 2 pounds whole mushrooms, cultivated and/or wild
- ½ cup olive oil
- 2 tablespoons unsalted butter, melted
- ½ teaspoon hot red-pepper flakes
- 2 teaspoons minced garlic
- ¼ cup dry white wine
- 1 teaspoon grated lemon rind
- ¼ cup minced green onions

1. Clean mushrooms with a brush or a damp paper towel; do not wash. In a large bowl whisk together oil, butter, red-pepper flakes, garlic, wine, and lemon rind. Add mushrooms, toss to coat well, and marinate 15 minutes at room temperature.

2. After removing skirt steak from the grill (see Bistecca recipe at left), arrange a large piece of heavy-duty foil atop the grate, turning up the edges to make a sort of pan. Remove mushrooms from their marinade, reserving marinade, and place them in foil pan. Cover grill and cook until hot throughout, 5 to 8 minutes. Remove foil and put mushrooms in a serving bowl with reserved marinade. Let cool to room temperature. Stir in green onions just before serving.

Serves 4.

Beat the summer heat with chilled Chianti and a Cold Supper: steak with fresh tomato sauce, grilled marinated mushrooms, salad, and a refreshing melon ice.

GRANITA DI MELONE
Melon ice

A typical Sicilian breakfast includes thick slices of golden brioche (see Pane di Mattina alla Siciliana, page 50), inky espresso—and melon ice! Americans might find it more suitable as a summer dessert, however, especially refreshing after a clambake or barbecue. Note that the melon must marinate at least 2 hours, and the blended mixture must chill for another 2 hours.

> 2 *pounds ripe melon (honeydew, cantaloupe, or Persian)*
> ⅓ *cup sugar*
> 1½ *tablespoons lemon juice*
> *Grated rind of 1 lemon*
> ¼ *teaspoon ground allspice*
> ¼ *teaspoon freshly ground black pepper (optional)*
> *Pinch of nutmeg*
> ½ *cup diced melon sprinkled with 2 tablespoons lemon juice or sweet white wine, for garnish*
> *Fresh mint sprigs, for garnish*

1. Peel melons, halve, and seed. Cut into chunks and put in stainless steel, glass, or ceramic bowl. Add sugar, lemon juice, lemon rind, allspice, pepper (if used), and nutmeg. Cover and marinate at room temperature for 2 hours, or refrigerate up to 12 hours.

2. Strain the accumulated juices into a small saucepan. Bring to a boil over high heat and cook 1 minute. Remove from heat and let cool. Combine marinated melon and reduced juices in a food processor or blender and blend until smooth. Chill for 2 hours.

3. Pour mixture into container of an ice cream freezer and freeze according to manufacturer's directions. Serve garnished with diced melon and fresh mint.

Serves 6 or 7.

VEGETABLES

Italians rarely serve vegetables on the same plate with meat, as Americans do. In an Italian meal the vegetable appears as a separate dish or as a separate course. Asparagi di Primavera (at right), for example, or Piselli al Prosciutto (see page 108) would certainly be served on their own before the main course. Even such a dish as Funghi Saltati (opposite page), although it goes wonderfully with red meats and game, might occasionally appear as a first course.

Among vegetable dishes that do usually accompany meat or fish are Spinaci con Pignoli (page 108) and Patate al Forno (below). A dish such as Melanzane alla Parmigiana (page 110) would probably be served separately in Italy, but in the context of an American meal it goes well as a side to roast chicken or lamb.

The dozen vegetable dishes that follow include both first-course and side-dish selections. Serving suggestions have been made with American dining habits in mind.

PATATE AL FORNO
Tuscan-style roasted potatoes

Crusty baked potato wedges get the royal Tuscan treatment: a basting of olive oil and a dusting of garlic and Parmesan. They're as divine with an American burger as they are with the traditional Bistecca alla Fiorentina (see page 76).

> 3 *large baking potatoes*
> ¾ *cup (approximately) olive oil*
> *Coarse salt*
> 1 *tablespoon minced garlic*
> 2 *tablespoons freshly grated Parmesan*

1. Preheat oven to 375° F. Wash potatoes, dry well, and quarter lengthwise. Coat a heavy baking sheet with oil; arrange potatoes on sheet. Rub them well all over with olive oil, then dust with salt. Bake, basting every 15 minutes with oil, until well browned and cooked through.

2. When potatoes are almost tender, heat ¼ cup olive oil in a small saucepan or skillet over moderately low heat. Add garlic and cook 1 minute, stirring constantly. Strain, setting garlic aside and reserving oil for another use.

3. Transfer potatoes to a warm serving platter; sprinkle with garlic and Parmesan. Serve immediately.

Serves 4.

ASPARAGI DI PRIMAVERA
Asparagus with lemon, tomato, and onions

When asparagus and the new onions turn up in the markets at the same time, the chefs of Bologna prepare this dish and put it in their windows.

> 1½ *pounds medium asparagus*
> 2 *small, sweet new onions or 4 green onions, minced*
> 2 *tablespoons lemon juice*
> ½ *cup extravirgin olive oil*
> *Grated rind of 1 lemon*
> 2 *tablespoons minced fresh chives*
> 2 *tomatoes, peeled, seeded, and diced (see page 29)*
> *Salt and freshly ground black pepper*

1. Bring a large pot of salted water to a boil. Add asparagus and cook until barely tender (about 5 minutes). Transfer with tongs to a bowl of ice water. When cool, drain and dry well. Transfer to a serving platter with all tips facing the same direction.

2. Combine onion, lemon juice, olive oil, lemon rind, and half of the chives. Whisk well, then stir in tomatoes. Season to taste with salt and pepper. Spoon sauce over asparagus, then garnish with remaining chives. Serve at room temperature.

Serves 4.

FUNGHI SALTATI
Mixed mushroom sauté

Northern Italians are avid stalkers of wild mushrooms, which their woods and mountains yield in abundance. Braised with garlic, cream, and herbs, mushrooms are the partner par excellence for roasted red meats, game, and fine wines.

1½ *pounds fresh wild mushrooms (porcini, chanterelles, morels, or oyster mushrooms)*
1 *pound small cultivated button mushrooms*
½ *cup butter*
1 *tablespoon olive oil*
3 *tablespoons minced garlic*
2 *tablespoons whipping cream*
   Salt and freshly ground black pepper
⅓ *cup minced mixed herbs (parsley, basil, chives, oregano)*

1. Clean mushrooms well with a mushroom brush or soft toothbrush; do not wash. Cut wild mushrooms into rough chunks about the size of the button mushrooms; leave button mushrooms whole.

2. Heat butter and olive oil in a large skillet over low heat. Add garlic and sauté one minute, stirring; do not allow garlic to color. Raise heat to high, add mushrooms and toss to coat with butter. Sauté quickly until mushrooms have softened, about 2 minutes. Add cream and cook until it is absorbed. Season to taste with salt and pepper. Add herbs, remove from heat, and transfer to a warm serving platter. Serve immediately.

Serves 4.

Potatoes Italian style: Cut them in wedges, bake with olive oil, then sprinkle with garlic and Parmesan. The resulting golden Patate al Forno can accompany any sturdy meat dish.

1. Pick over spinach carefully and discard any large, tough outer leaves or bruised leaves. Leave inner leaves attached to their tender stems. Wash well and dry.

2. Heat olive oil in a large sauté pan over moderately low heat. Add garlic and sauté about 30 seconds, stirring constantly. Raise heat to medium-high. Add spinach and salt to taste. Sauté, turning spinach over constantly with tongs, for about 25 seconds or until spinach just wilts. Reduce heat to low, add pine nuts and raisins. Cook an additional 15 seconds. Drizzle lemon juice over dish and season to taste with pepper. Taste and add more salt if needed. Serve immediately.

Serves 4.

PISELLI AL PROSCIUTTO
Peas with prosciutto

The first June peas usually turn up in Roman restaurants stewed with butter, prosciutto, and green onions. They're always served as a separate first course, with bread to mop up the buttery juices.

>   5   *pounds fresh peas*
>   6   *tablespoons butter*
>   ½   *cup green onions, in*
>   *pea-size dice*
>   1   *cup unsalted homemade*
>   *chicken stock*
>   1   *cup paper-thin julienned*
>   *prosciutto*
>   2   *tablespoons minced green*
>   *onions, white part only, for*
>   *garnish*

Shell peas. Melt butter in a sauté pan over moderately low heat. Add diced green onions and cook 2 minutes. Add peas and stock; cook until peas are just tender, about 8 to 10 minutes. Stir in prosciutto and remove from heat. Top with minced green onions and serve immediately.

Serves 6.

Braise the first June peas the Roman way—with scallions and sliced prosciutto—and serve as a first course before a roast spring lamb.

SPINACI CON PIGNOLI
Wilted spinach with pine nuts and raisins

Barely wilted spinach seasoned with garlic, pine nuts, and lemon is a side dish that fits in just about anywhere. Sicilian cooks add golden raisins and serve it with grilled tuna or swordfish; you might also serve it with Pollo alla Diavola (see page 93), Fagotini di Pollo con Cipolle Balsamiche (see page 88), Saltimbocca (see page 84), or Arrosto di Maiale al Latte (see page 85).

>   3   *bunches spinach*
>   3   *tablespoons olive oil*
>   2   *teaspoons minced garlic*
>   *Coarse salt*
>   ¼   *cup toasted pine nuts*
>   2   *tablespoons golden raisins*
>   2   *tablespoons lemon juice*
>   *Freshly ground black pepper*

POMODORI DELL' ESTATE
Summer tomato casserole

If you drive through Italy in the height of summer, you might think you're seeing more tomatoes than the world can consume. The country seems to be bursting with them, but they all eventually get used, some in simple, rustic concoctions like this one. The dish depends on great tomatoes and good oil for its success. Serve it with herbed roast chicken, grilled fish, or lamb.

- ⅓ cup extravirgin olive oil
- ½ large red onion, sliced in ⅓-inch rounds
- 1½ large tomatoes, sliced ⅓ inch thick
  Salt and freshly ground black pepper
- ⅓ cup chopped fresh basil
- 4 garlic cloves, thinly slivered
- 2 small green zucchini, cut in ¼-inch dice
- 1 small yellow zucchini, cut in ¼-inch dice
- 3 tablespoons freshly grated Parmesan

1. Preheat oven to 350° F. Using 2 tablespoons of the oil, coat the bottom and sides of a small baking dish, about 8 by 6 inches. Line bottom with onion slices; do not let slices overlap. Top with half of the tomato slices, a little salt and pepper, and half of the basil. Insert half of the garlic slivers in tomatoes. Drizzle with half of the remaining oil.

2. Repeat with another layer of tomato slices, salt and pepper, basil, and garlic. Combine the diced squashes and strew over the top. Drizzle with remaining oil and dust with Parmesan. Cover and bake 35 minutes. Cool slightly before serving directly from the casserole.

Serves 4.

MELANZANE FRITTE
Deep-fried eggplant

One of the charms of eggplant is how readily it absorbs other flavors. Layer it with garlic, vinegar, and basil, and it will be heavenly in a matter of hours. The slender Japanese eggplants sliced into fans make a clever, if nontraditional, presentation. Serve the dish as a summer first course with Bruschetta (see page 13), or offer it as a side dish with grilled lamb or poultry.

- 8 small, long Japanese eggplants
  Olive oil and safflower oil, for deep-frying
  Coarse salt
- ¼ cup minced garlic
- ½ cup minced fresh basil
- ¼ cup red wine vinegar

1. Wash and dry eggplants; do not peel. Cut eggplants into "fans": Starting at broad end, cut them lengthwise into slices about ⅓ inch thick, being careful not to cut through the stem.

2. Heat oil in a large deep kettle or deep-fryer. Use 1 part olive oil to 3 parts safflower oil. When oil reaches 350° F, add half the eggplants and fry until they float and are soft, about 4 to 6 minutes. Remove immediately with a slotted spoon to a stainless steel, glass, or ceramic bowl. Dust with salt and sprinkle with half of the garlic and half of the basil.

3. Repeat with remaining eggplants, transferring them to the same bowl as they are done and sprinkling them with salt and the remaining garlic and basil. Sprinkle vinegar over top and let vegetables cool to room temperature. Cover and refrigerate 6 to 8 hours or overnight.

4. To serve, bring eggplants to room temperature. Transfer to a serving platter with a lip and pour any marinade over them.

Serves 4.

CARCIOFI FRITTI CON CIPOLLE
Artichoke and onion sauté

This northern Italian dish is quickly made and great with veal and lamb. Use leftover artichokes in a frittata or as a simple topping for pasta.

- 3 medium artichokes
- 1 lemon, halved
- 2 tablespoons butter
- 2 tablespoons olive oil
- ½ cup minced onion
- 2 tablespoons chopped fresh oregano
- ½ cup white wine
- 2 tablespoons drained small capers
  Coarse salt and freshly ground black pepper
  Additional lemon (optional)

1. Remove the tough, dark green outer leaves of the artichokes. Trim the stems and cut off the top third of the artichokes with a serrated knife. Quarter the artichokes and remove the fuzzy choke. Rub all cut surfaces with a lemon half. Transfer to a bowl of cold water acidulated with the juice of half a lemon.

2. In a large sauté pan, heat butter and olive oil over moderately low heat. Add onion and cook gently until softened but not browned. Drain artichokes in a colander, then add to sauté pan. Turn heat to high to sear them quickly, shaking pan constantly. Add oregano, wine, capers, and salt and pepper to taste. Reduce heat to low, cover partially, and simmer 8 minutes. Uncover and cook until almost all the liquid has evaporated and artichokes are tender. Taste and add more salt or pepper if needed. Add a squeeze of lemon juice if desired. Transfer to a serving bowl and serve immediately.

Serves 4.

CARCIOFI ALLA ROMANA
Herb-steamed artichokes, Roman style

In Rome artichokes are bathed in oil, then baked with garlic, herbs, and wine until fragrant and tender. They are a delicious first course on their own, with sturdy bread to soak up the juices, but they're equally good as a buffet dish or as part of an antipasto.

- 4 medium artichokes
- 1 lemon, halved
- 4 large cloves garlic, minced
- ¼ cup chopped fresh basil
- 2 tablespoons minced parsley
- 2 teaspoons coarse salt
- 1½ teaspoons freshly ground black pepper
- ½ cup plus 2 tablespoons olive oil
- ¼ cup white wine
  Additional 2 tablespoons minced mixed basil and parsley, for garnish

1. Remove the tough, dark green outer leaves of the artichokes. Trim the stems and cut off the top third of the artichokes with a serrated knife. Quarter the artichokes and remove the fuzzy choke. Rub all cut surfaces with a lemon half. Transfer to a bowl of cold water acidulated with the juice of half a lemon.

2. Preheat oven to 350° F. In a bowl, combine garlic, basil, parsley, salt, and pepper. Whisk in the ½ cup oil. Drain artichokes, pat them dry, and add to the bowl. Turn to coat well with oil.

3. Transfer artichokes and their marinade to a baking dish, overlapping the pieces slightly. Sprinkle wine around the corners of the dish. Drizzle with the remaining oil. Cover dish tightly with aluminum foil and bake 30 minutes. Check artichokes for tenderness. When they are done, a small, sharp knife will pierce them easily. Continue cooking until tender. Remove to a serving platter and garnish with additional basil-parsley mixture. Serve hot or at room temperature.

Serves 4.

CAVOLO DI VENEZIA CON PANCETTA
Cabbage with pancetta, Venetian style

Venetians braise cabbage with *pancetta* and garlic, then spike it with wine vinegar. With a bowl of steaming polenta (see page 58), this dish makes a humble but wonderful supper. Any leftovers can be the beginning of a delicious frittata.

- 6 ounces pancetta, cut in small cubes
- 1 tablespoon olive oil
- 4 tablespoons butter
- ¾ cup minced onion
- 1 tablespoon minced garlic
- 8 cups shredded cabbage
  Salt and freshly ground black pepper
- 3 tablespoons red or white wine vinegar
- 2 tablespoons minced Italian parsley, for garnish

1. In a large saucepan or small stockpot over moderately low heat, fry pancetta cubes slowly until crisp. Transfer with a slotted spoon to a small bowl. Pour off all but 1 tablespoon of fat. Add olive oil and 2 tablespoons of the butter to the pan. When butter has melted and fats are hot, add onion and garlic. Sauté gently over low heat until softened but not browned, about 5 minutes.

2. Add cabbage to pan and turn to coat well with oil. Add rendered pancetta, salt and pepper to taste, and vinegar. Top with remaining butter, cut in small pieces. Cover and cook over moderately low heat until cabbage is almost "melted," about 1 hour. Taste and add more salt or pepper if needed. Garnish with parsley and serve immediately.

Serves 4.

CIME DI RAPE ALLA ROMANA
Roman-style broccoli raab

The flavorful broccoli raab (sometimes called *rape* or *broccoletti di rape*), loved and served all over Italy, can be found in this country as well. Its full flavor stands up to garlic and cheese and is an excellent foil for pork or tomato-sauce dishes. Substitute Swiss chard if it is unavailable.

- 2 pounds broccoli raab
- ¼ cup olive oil
- ½ tablespoon minced garlic
  Coarse salt and freshly ground black pepper
- 3 tablespoons lemon juice
- 2 tablespoons grated Romano cheese

1. Wash broccoli raab and trim away any woody stems. Bring a large pot of salted water to a boil. Blanch broccoli raab 2 minutes. Drain and refresh in a bowl of ice water. Drain again and gently towel-dry.

2. Heat olive oil in a large skillet over moderate heat. Add garlic and sauté, stirring constantly, 1 minute. Add broccoli and cook, turning often with tongs, until greens are coated with oil, hot throughout, and tender, about 2 minutes. Season to taste with salt and pepper; add lemon juice. Transfer to a warm serving platter. Dust with cheese and serve at once.

Serves 4.

MELANZANE ALLA PARMIGIANA
Eggplant Parma style

An elegant eggplant Parmigiana is definitely not a contradiction in terms. When the eggplant is fried without breading and layered with a lively sauce, prosciutto, and peppers, the result is a vibrant dish that's appropriate for company meals. It's equally tasty at room temperature and is thus well suited to buffets. For a more formal, dinner-party presentation, bake the dish in individual ramekins. Note that the eggplant must stand 2 hours.

2 large eggplants (about 1 to 1¼ lb each)
   Coarse salt

1 cup light olive oil

6 ounces prosciutto, sliced paper-thin

1 large red onion, sliced paper-thin

1 recipe Roasted Red Peppers (see page 14)

⅓ cup freshly grated Parmesan plus ¼ cup for garnish

1 teaspoon freshly ground black pepper

1½ cups Sugo di Pomodoro (see page 36)

3 tablespoons minced parsley, for garnish

1. Wash and dry eggplants; slice into rounds about ½ inch thick. Place rounds on baking sheets lined with paper towels. Sprinkle with salt and let stand 2 hours to draw out the bitter juices. Pat dry.

2. Preheat oven to 350° F. Using ¼ cup olive oil at a time, fry eggplant slices on both sides in a large skillet over moderately high heat. Blot them lightly on paper towels and set aside.

3. Using an 11- by 13-inch baking pan, make layers as follows: eggplant slices, then prosciutto, then onion, then a few red pepper strips, then a light dusting of Parmesan and a sprinkling of pepper, then one third of the tomato sauce. Repeat two times, ending with tomato sauce. Bake 35 minutes, or until bubbling hot throughout. Dust top with additional Parmesan and parsley. Cool slightly before serving directly from the baking dish.

Serves 4 generously.

Make-Ahead Tip The dish can be assembled a day in advance, then covered and refrigerated. Bring to room temperature before baking.

Melanzane alla Parmigiana can be a fit-for-company dish when made with roasted red peppers and prosciutto. The eggplant is fried without breading to keep the flavors and textures light.

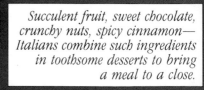

*Succulent fruit, sweet chocolate,
crunchy nuts, spicy cinnamon—
Italians combine such ingredients
in toothsome desserts to bring
a meal to a close.*

Desserts

Although the most common Italian dessert is fruit, such as wine-marinated peaches (see Pesche al Vino, page 114), luscious cakes and other sweets are not unknown. In this chapter you'll find the familiar Zabaglione (see page 119) and Biscuit Tortoni (see page 120), a fig tart (see Crostata di Frutta alla Panna, page 118), rich Torta di Ricotta (see page 114), and Italian ices (see page 117). A special note on *caffè* (see page 118) explains the many forms in which Italians drink this beverage, and the chapter concludes with a magnificent dessert buffet (see page 120).

DESSERTS

Except on holidays and other special occasions, Italian meals rarely end with a rich dessert. Fresh fruit, fruit and cheese, or desserts based on fruit—like Pesche al Vino (at right) or Fichi al Forno (see page 118)— are far more common than elaborate pastries or cakes. Ice cream (*gelato*) is a popular midafternoon pick-me-up, usually purchased by the cup from a street vendor. Cakes such as Torta di Ricotta (at right) or Torta del Re (see page 119) might be offered in the late afternoon with a glass of sweet wine.

TORTA DI POLENTA
Polenta pound cake

Use this golden loaf cake as the basis of a delectable strawberry shortcake: Slice it and toast it, then top it with berries and cream. Sugar the berries an hour or so before serving to draw out their juices. The use of polenta marks this as a northern Italian dish.

- 6 ounces unsalted butter, softened
- ⅔ cup sugar
- 2 eggs
- 1½ cups flour
- ½ cup semolina
- ⅔ cup polenta
- 2 teaspoons baking powder
- 1 teaspoon baking soda
- ½ teaspoon salt
- 1 cup buttermilk
  Sugar, for dusting pan
  Fresh raspberries, sliced strawberries, or sliced figs
  Lightly whipped and sweetened cream

1. Preheat oven to 375° F. In a large mixing bowl, cream butter until light. Add sugar gradually and beat until light and fluffy. Beat in eggs one at a time and mix thoroughly.

2. Sift together flour, semolina, polenta, baking powder, baking soda, and salt. Add to creamed mixture in three parts, alternating with buttermilk. Beat just to blend.

3. Butter a 9-inch loaf pan; sprinkle bottom and sides with sugar, shaking out excess. Pour in batter and bake until a tester inserted in the center comes out clean, about 1 hour. Cool completely on a rack before serving. Slice and serve with fruit and whipped cream.

Makes one 9-inch loaf.

PESCHE AL VINO
Peaches in Chianti

In Tuscany the local red wine is used to marinate thick-sliced peaches, producing a simple and supremely refreshing summer dessert. Choose a young and inexpensive Chianti and peaches that are fragrant but not overly soft.

- 8 medium to large freestone peaches, ripe but firm
- 2 tablespoons lemon juice
- 3 tablespoons sugar
- 1 bottle (750 ml) Chianti Biscotti per il Vino (see page 92)

Peel peaches and cut into eighths. Place in a stainless steel, glass, or ceramic bowl. Add lemon and sugar and mix gently but well. Let stand 5 minutes. Pour wine over peaches and cover. Refrigerate 8 hours or overnight. To serve arrange peach segments in wine glasses or wide-mouthed dessert glasses and spoon a little wine into each glass. Serve with *biscotti.*

Serves 8.

TORTA DI RICOTTA
Ricotta cheesecake

Cheesecakes in southern Italy are made with ricotta, raisins, and pine nuts and are commonly flecked with chocolate and flavored with rum. The version below incorporates crunchy pine-nut brittle, a delicious candy to savor on its own. Offer this rich *torta* in the afternoon with a glass of Marsala, or serve it as the luscious finish to a light meal.

- 1 cup superfine sugar
- 3 tablespoons water
- 5 tablespoons pine nuts
- 4 tablespoons golden raisins
- 2 tablespoons rum
- 3¼ cups flour
- 1 tablespoon baking powder
- ½ cup dark brown sugar
- 1¼ cups ground almonds
- 8 ounces chilled, unsalted butter, in small pieces
- 1 egg
- 1 teaspoon vanilla extract
- 1½ pounds whole-milk ricotta
- 1 teaspoon grated lemon rind
- 2 ounces milk chocolate, coarsely chopped

1. In a 1-quart saucepan, heat ¼ cup of the superfine sugar and the water over high heat. When mixture boils and sugar dissolves, add pine nuts. Continue cooking, swirling pan often, until sugar turns a light brown. Turn out mixture onto an oiled baking sheet and let cool. Break up into small chunks.

2. Combine raisins and rum in a small bowl and set aside for 1 hour.

3. *To make dough in a food processor:* Combine flour, baking powder, brown sugar, and almonds in workbowl of food processor. Process 5 seconds. Add butter and process until mixture resembles coarse meal, about 10 seconds. Whisk egg and vanilla together, then add to food processor with motor running. Process just until dough nearly holds

together. Turn out dough onto a board and gather into a ball; do not knead or work the dough, even if it doesn't hold together well. Wrap in plastic and refrigerate at least 1 hour. *To make dough by hand:* Stir together flour, baking powder, brown sugar, and almonds. Cut in butter with two knives or a pastry blender until mixture resembles coarse meal. Whisk egg and vanilla together, then add to flour mixture. Toss lightly with a fork, just until dough holds together. Gather into a ball; do not knead or work the dough, even if it doesn't hold together well. Wrap in plastic and refrigerate at least 1 hour.

4. In a large bowl, combine ricotta, the remaining superfine sugar, lemon rind, raisins, and rum. Add chocolate pieces and pine-nut brittle; mix well.

5. Preheat oven to 350° F. Line bottom and sides of a 10-inch springform baking pan with foil. Place a little more than half of the dough on the bottom of the pan, patting it into place and pushing it partway up the sides. Spoon in ricotta filling; roll out remaining pastry into a 10-inch round and lay it over the top of the filling. Bake 50 to 55 minutes; top will color slightly.

6. Transfer cheesecake to a rack and cool in the pan. Release sides of springform pan and gently peel back the foil from the sides. Lift the bottom of the cake gently with a spatula and pull out the foil. Serve barely warm or at room temperature.

Makes one 10-inch cheesecake.

Make-Ahead Tip Pastry dough may be made a day ahead and refrigerated.

Torta di Ricotta is cheesecake made the southern Italian way, with a ricotta filling encased in pastry. Raisins, pine nuts, almonds, and a hint of chocolate enrich the filling.

Make creamy Gelato d'Albicocca with dried apricots and apricot brandy for a winter reminder of a favorite summer fruit. Cookies and espresso partner it well.

GELATO DI CAFFÈ
Espresso ice cream

The dark-roasted beans that make such strong, rich coffee are often used to flavor ice cream, too. In fact, Gelato di Caffè is a favorite of all Italians who like ice cream—which is to say, it's a favorite of all Italians.

- ¼ cup very finely ground (espresso grind) espresso coffee beans
- 1 cup half-and-half
- ½ cup milk
- 1½ cups whipping cream (preferably not ultrapasteurized)
- 5 egg yolks
- 1 cup sugar
  Cocoa powder or ground cinnamon, for garnish (optional)
- 8 chocolate-coated espresso beans, for garnish (optional)

1. Put ground coffee in paper-lined coffee filter as if making drip coffee. Set filter over a bowl. Combine half-and-half and milk in a small saucepan and scald. Pour milk mixture over coffee grounds and let drip; it may take up to 15 minutes to drip through. Pour filtered milk-coffee mixture back into saucepan, add whipping cream, and set pan over low heat.

2. Combine egg yolks and sugar in a bowl and whisk until they form a "ribbon" when the whisk is lifted. Add warm cream to egg yolks in a steady stream and whisk to blend. Pour mixture back into saucepan and set over low heat. Cook, stirring constantly with a wooden spoon, until mixture thickens slightly and coats the spoon. Do not allow to boil. Remove from heat and let cool to room temperature.

3. Transfer mixture to an ice cream freezer and freeze according to manufacturer's directions. Serve as is or with a dust with sifted cocoa powder or cinnamon. If desired, garnish each serving with a chocolate-coated espresso bean.

Serves 8.

GELATO D'ALBICOCCA
Apricot ice cream

This creamy dessert from Rome is extremely rich and should be proffered in small portions. A dainty demitasse makes an elegant serving dish. Note that the mixture needs to chill for a day before freezing.

- 8 egg yolks
- 1 tablespoon sugar
  Grated rind of 1 lemon
- 2¼ cups whipping cream
- ¼ teaspoon almond extract
- 1½ teaspoons ground cinnamon
- 1¾ cups minced dried apricots
- ¼ cup apricot brandy
- ½ cup water
- 8 ounces thick apricot preserves
- 1 tablespoon lemon juice

1. Combine egg yolks and sugar in top of double boiler. Set over, but not in, simmering water and whisk well. Add lemon rind and cream, then cook, whisking constantly, until mixture is slightly thickened and has reached 180° F. Remove from heat. Add almond extract and cinnamon.

2. Combine apricots, brandy, and water in a small saucepan. Bring to a boil over high heat and boil until no liquid remains and apricots are very soft. Add apricots to cream mixture.

3. Combine preserves and lemon juice in a small saucepan. Cook, stirring, over moderately low heat until preserves become thin and runny. Remove from heat, cool slightly, and add to cream mixture. Cool to room temperature, then cover and refrigerate 24 hours. Transfer mixture to an ice cream freezer and freeze according to manufacturer's directions. Store ice cream in freezer for at least 1 hour before serving.

Makes about 6 cups, 12 to 14 small servings.

Make-Ahead Tip The ice cream keeps up to 1 week.

TORTA DI RISO
Italian rice cake

The stubby, short-grain, Arborio rice that makes the creamy *risotti* of Piedmont (see page 61) is also turned into sweet rice puddings. Enriched with dried fruits and nuts and enlivened with citrus peel, a warm Torta di Riso is a winter dessert best accompanied by Asti Spumante.

- ½ cup hazelnut- or almond-flavored liqueur
- 4¼ cups water
- ½ cup each golden raisins, dried currants, minced dried figs, and Italian Arborio rice
- 4 cups milk
  Grated rind of 1 lemon
  Grated rind of ½ orange
- ¾ cup sugar plus sugar for dusting pan
- 6 eggs
- ¾ cup chopped almonds
- 1 teaspoon almond extract
  Butter, for greasing pan

1. Combine liqueur, ¼ cup of the water, raisins, currants, and figs in a small saucepan. Bring to a simmer over medium heat and let simmer 5 minutes. Set aside until all liquid is absorbed (this may take a few hours).

2. In a medium saucepan over high heat, bring the remaining water to a boil. Add rice and cook 3 minutes. Drain, then return rice to a clean saucepan with milk, lemon rind, and orange rind. Bring to a simmer over moderately high heat, then reduce heat to low, cover, and cook 1 hour. Remove from heat, cool, and add sugar. Add eggs one at a time, blending well, then stir in nuts, almond extract, and fruit mixture.

3. Preheat oven to 325° F. Butter bottom and sides of a 9-inch round cake pan, then coat with sugar, shaking out excess. Pour batter into prepared pan. Bake until a knife inserted in center comes out clean, about 1 hour. Remove cake to a rack; cool in pan. To serve, turn cake out of pan and cut into wedges. Serve warm, at room temperature, or cold.

Serves 8.

COFFEE, ITALIAN STYLE

The bittersweet flavor of strong Italian coffee is an acquired taste for many Americans. For most Italians, however, it is a pleasure indulged in daily, sometimes several times a day.

Inky-dark espresso, served in small cups, is always offered at the end of a restaurant meal. Espresso is made by forcing water under considerable pressure through dark-roasted, tightly packed coffee grounds. The resulting brew is bitter and rich, a welcome jolt that prepares one for the rest of the day's or evening's activities. Some hardy souls request a *doppio* (double) or an added splash of grappa or anisette.

Few Italian homes are equipped with the powerful steam-generating machines required to make a true espresso. At home, the after-dinner coffee is usually made in a *napoletana*, a three-part coffeepot that sits on the stove burner. Water goes into the bottom part, and coffee into a basket in the middle. The top part, which has a spout, is screwed on spout side down. When the water in the bottom begins to steam, the whole contraption is turned upside down to allow the hot water to drip through. The coffee is dark, rich, and less bitter than a steam-made espresso.

Coffee is not reserved for the end of a meal, however. Most Italians begin their morning with a cup of coffee, too. And in the middle of the afternoon, when a pause or a pick-me-up is desired, Italians gather in caffès for coffee, conversation, and a little something sweet.

Although everyone drinks espresso after meals, in the morning and mid-afternoon many Italians prefer a gentler brew. *Caffè latte*—one part espresso to three parts steamed milk—is a particularly soothing morning beverage. Cappuccino—one part espresso to two parts steamed milk, the top sometimes dusted with chocolate—makes a delicious and satisfying afternoon treat.

CROSTATA DI FRUTTA ALLA PANNA
Fruit tart with cream

This Tuscan tart is easy to make and as humble as an apple dumpling. Dried fruits are stewed with Marsala and grappa, then puréed, spread in a tart shell, and topped with soft Crème Fraîche. Wedges of ripe fresh figs make a handsome garnish. For best results, fill and garnish tart shell just before serving.

> 1 cup flour
>   Pinch of salt
> 5 tablespoons chilled, unsalted butter
> 3 tablespoons ice water
> 6 ounces dried figs, stems removed
> 2 ounces dried apricots
> 2 tablespoons Marsala
> 1 tablespoon grappa or brandy
> 1 tablespoon honey
> 2 tablespoons water
> ¼ cup Crème Fraîche (see page 123)
> 2 large fresh figs, for garnish

1. Stir together flour and salt. Cut in butter until mixture resembles coarse crumbs. Add ice water and toss with a fork until mixture begins to come together. Quickly form it into a smooth ball, wrap in waxed paper, and chill 15 minutes.

2. In a saucepan combine figs, apricots, Marsala, grappa, honey, and 2 tablespoons water. Bring to a boil, reduce heat to maintain a simmer, and cook 15 minutes to soften the fruit. Set aside to cool.

3. Preheat oven to 375° F. Roll out dough on a lightly floured surface to a round ⅛ inch thick. Transfer to a 10-inch tart pan and press dough onto the bottom and sides. Trim away any excess. Prick well all over with a fork. Cover surface with foil and weight with rice or beans. Bake 10 minutes, then remove foil and rice and bake until golden and crisp, another 12 to 15 minutes. Cool tart shell on a rack.

4. Put cooled fruit mixture into food processor or blender and blend until smooth. Lightly whip the Crème Fraîche. Put puréed fruit mixture in cooled tart shell. Spread a thin layer of Crème Fraîche over the purée. Cut fresh figs into thin wedges and arrange attractively atop the tart.

Makes one 10-inch tart.

FICHI AL FORNO
Roasted figs

Ripe, fresh figs baked with butter, lemon, and honey are one of the easiest and most delectable of summer desserts. They are a specialty of Agropoli, an ancient Greek settlement on Italy's Amalfi coast. Serve with a pitcher of heavy cream or a small scoop of vanilla ice cream.

> 3 tablespoons butter
> 2 tablespoons honey
> 8 fresh figs, halved through the stem end
> 4 tablespoons bitter lemon marmalade
> 1 tablespoon brown sugar
> 1 teaspoon ground cinnamon
> 16 perfect walnut halves
> 2 tablespoons grated lemon rind, for garnish

1. Preheat oven to 350° F. Coat bottom of a 13- by 9-inch glass baking dish with 1 tablespoon of the butter. Pour in honey and spread it over the bottom of the dish with a spatula. Place dish in oven to melt the honey, about 10 minutes.

2. Add figs to baking dish, skin side down. Dot with the remaining butter and top each half with a dollop of marmalade. Combine brown sugar and cinnamon and sprinkle over figs. Top each with a walnut half. Bake until figs are hot and honey begins to caramelize, about 12 minutes. Serve warm, garnished with lemon rind.

Serves 8.

TORTA DEL RE
King's cake

Serve this sweet with small cups of steaming espresso. For a more elaborate dessert, add seasonal fruit and a bowl of fresh ricotta. Torta del Re comes from Friuli, a region in northern Italy adjacent to Yugoslavia.

- 1 cup unsalted butter, at room temperature
- ⅔ cup honey
- 2 eggs
- 1 cup flour
- ½ cup coarsely chopped dried figs
- ½ cup toasted pine nuts

Preheat oven to 325° F. In a large mixing bowl, cream butter. Add honey and beat until light. Beat in eggs one at a time, mixing well. Add flour gradually, beating until smooth. Stir in figs and nuts. Place dough in a 9-inch square baking dish and bake until tester inserted in center comes out clean, about 40 minutes. Cool on a rack; serve warm or at room temperature, in small squares.

Makes one 9-inch square cake.

ZABAGLIONE
Italian wine custard

The strong arm of a professional chef can whip eggs and wine to an airy foam in less than a minute. The confident home cook can do the same, but less experienced whisk-wielders may want to use electric beaters. Serve the frothy warm custard with crunchy Biscotti per il Vino (see page 92) for textural contrast, or spoon it over sliced strawberries. Although Zabaglione is made only with the Marsala wine of Sicily, it is enjoyed all over Italy.

- 4 egg yolks
- 3 tablespoons superfine sugar
- ½ cup Marsala

In the bottom of a double boiler over high heat, bring water to a boil. Reduce heat to maintain a bare simmer. Put egg yolks and sugar in top of double boiler and set over, but not in, simmering water. Whisk by hand or with electric beaters until mixture thickens slightly and begins to turn pale. Add Marsala and continue whisking until mixture doubles in volume and is very smooth and fluffy. Serve immediately.

Serves 5 or 6.

Dried apricots and figs make a sweet, smooth filling for a winter Crostata di Frutta alla Panna. Top with silky Crème Fraîche and a dried fig cut in half.

119

A DESSERT BUFFET

Torta di Pere

Biscuit Tortoni

Budino di Mascarpone

Cassata Donna Lugata

Panini di Gelato

Gelato di Limone

For a bridal shower, an afternoon tea, or an end to an evening of theater, consider offering your guests an elaborate dessert buffet. Set the ice cream container in a wine bucket surrounded by ice and let guests serve themselves; all the other desserts can be arranged individually on trays. To give guests a chance to try everything, you might want to reduce portion sizes from those indicated in the recipes. The Cassata, for example, may be made in thirty-six 1½-inch miniature cupcake tins. Offer coffee, tea, and an Italian sweet wine or a chilled Asti Spumante.

TORTA DI PERE
Tuscan pear cake

This rustic country cake can be on the table within an hour and is best shortly after it's made. Bosc pears are recommended as they hold their shape when baked, but other pears or even apples could be substituted.

2 tablespoons butter
⅓ cup fine amaretti crumbs or stale cake or cookie crumbs
1 pound ripe Bosc pears
⅓ cup dark rum
4 eggs
1½ cups granulated sugar
3 cups flour
2 teaspoons baking powder
½ teaspoon salt
¼ cup confectioners' sugar

1. Preheat oven to 350° F. Grease an 8-inch springform pan with butter; dust all over with *amaretti* crumbs.

2. Quarter unpeeled pears; core them and cut them into slices ⅛ inch thick. Put slices in a ceramic, glass, or stainless steel bowl and add rum. Toss gently to blend and set aside for a few minutes.

3. Beat eggs and granulated sugar in an electric mixer on high speed until light and fluffy. Sift together flour, baking powder, and salt. Fold flour mixture into egg mixture by hand. Place half the pear slices on the bottom of the prepared pan; cover with batter and arrange the remaining pear slices on top. Bake 20 minutes; quickly dust top with confectioners' sugar and return to oven until cake is well browned and a tester inserted in the center comes out clean, about another 20 minutes. Serve warm.

Serves 4 to 6.

BISCUIT TORTONI
Frozen almond cream

The original Biscuit Tortoni debuted in 1798, the creation of a Neapolitan (Signor Tortoni) who owned a Parisian ice cream shop. The clever Tortoni used crushed *amaretti* (almond macaroons) to flavor a frozen cream. It delighted Parisians and even today is probably better known outside than within Italy. Restaurants and dinner-party hosts love it because it's elegant and easy, and because it must be made ahead. Use the commercially available amaretti to make crumbs.

¾ cup half-and-half
¾ cup medium-fine amaretti crumbs
2 tablespoons confectioners' sugar
  Grated rind of 1 orange
3 tablespoons golden raisins
  Pinch of salt
½ cup whipping cream
½ cup Crème Fraîche (see page 123)
½ teaspoon almond extract
¼ cup slivered blanched almonds, for garnish
  Fresh mint leaves, for garnish

1. In a large bowl, combine half-and-half, amaretti crumbs, sugar, orange rind, raisins, and salt. Let stand at room temperature 1 hour.

2. In a large bowl, whip cream lightly to soft peaks; fold in Crème Fraîche and almond extract, then fold in amaretti mixture. Divide mixture among four goblets or ramekins and freeze for 3 to 4 hours.

3. Preheat oven to 350° F. Toast almonds until lightly browned and fragrant. Just before serving, garnish each Biscuit Tortoni with hot toasted almonds and a mint leaf.

Serves 4.

A sampling of Italy's sweet specialties (top to bottom): Biscuit Tortoni, Budino di Mascarpone, Panini di Gelato, Torta di Pere, and Cassata Donna Lugata.

BUDINO DI MASCARPONE
Mascarpone pudding

Cream cheese will work in this souf-fléed pudding, but look hard for *mascarpone* (see page 20); it has a buttery, nutty richness that cream cheese doesn't match. Serve this northern Italian dessert with espresso or sweet wine and offer a plate of Dolci di Polenta (see page 72) or some far-from-Italian ginger snaps.

- 2 *tablespoons unsalted butter, melted*
  Sugar, for dusting
- 2 *tablespoons dried currants*
- 2 *tablespoons golden raisins*
- 2 *moist dried figs, coarsely chopped*
- 3 *tablespoons light rum*
- 1 *cup whole-milk ricotta, well drained*
- 5 *ounces mascarpone or natural cream cheese*
- 4 *eggs, separated*
- ¼ *cup flour*
- ½ *cup sugar*
- 1 *teaspoon cinnamon*
  Pinch of nutmeg
- ½ *teaspoon salt*
- 3 *tablespoons dark rum*

1. Brush melted butter on bottom and sides of a 2-quart soufflé dish or four 1½-cup individual soufflé dishes. Dust bottom and sides with sugar, shaking out excess. Set aside.

2. Preheat oven to 350° F. In a small bowl, combine currants, raisins, figs, and light rum. Stir to blend and set aside to marinate for at least 15 minutes.

3. In a large bowl, combine ricotta and mascarpone. Beat well; add egg yolks one at a time, beating well after each addition. Sift together flour, sugar, cinnamon, nutmeg, and salt. Add to cheese mixture and beat well. Fold in marinated fruit mixture.

4. Beat egg whites until stiff but not dry and gently fold into cheese mixture. Transfer mixture to soufflé dish(es); bake until nicely risen and firm to the touch, but not stiff. A 2-quart soufflé takes about 30 minutes; smaller soufflés cook faster. Quickly and gently brush the tops with dark rum. Serve hot or at room temperature. Pudding will deflate slightly as it cools.

Serves 4.

CASSATA DONNA LUGATA
Individual Sicilian cheesecakes

Lemon, cinnamon, and sweet Marsala flavor these miniature cheesecakes, with a drizzle of dark chocolate on top. Dress them up with paper-lined silver foil muffin cups.

- 1½ *pounds whole-milk ricotta or baker's cheese*
- 8 *ounces natural cream cheese*
- ½ *cup sugar*
- 2 *eggs*
- 1 *teaspoon grated lemon rind*
- 1 *teaspoon ground cinnamon*
  Pinch of nutmeg
- 2 *tablespoons Marsala*
- 4½ *ounces extra-bittersweet chocolate, melted and cooled slightly*

Sweet Dough

- 1¾ *cups flour*
- ½ *cup sugar*
- ¾ *teaspoon baking powder*
  Pinch of salt
- 6 *tablespoons chilled unsalted butter*
- 1 *egg, lightly beaten*
- 1 *teaspoon vanilla extract*

1. Preheat oven to 400° F. In a mixer or food processor, combine ricotta, cream cheese, sugar, and eggs. Beat well or process until well blended. Add lemon rind, cinnamon, nutmeg, and Marsala and beat or process until combined. Refrigerate mixture while making Sweet Dough.

2. Form Sweet Dough into a ball, then divide ball in half. Divide each half into 9 pieces, then roll each piece on a lightly floured surface into a 3-inch round. Line 18 muffin tins with paper cups, then press a dough round into each cup, pressing dough about a quarter of the way up the sides. Spoon chilled filling into dough cups.

3. Drizzle ½ tablespoon of melted chocolate over each cupcake and bake until well-browned and slightly puffed, about 20 minutes. Cool cakes on a rack and serve from their paper holders, either at room temperature or chilled.

Makes 18 little cakes.

Sweet Dough Sift together flour, sugar, baking powder, and salt. Cut in butter until mixture resembles coarse crumbs. Combine egg and vanilla, then add to dry mixture and toss with a fork until dough begins to hold together.

PANINI DI GELATO
Ice cream sandwiches

You may never find this creation in Italy, although its basic parts are Italian. California chef David Beckwith provided the original inspiration; fine cook Derna Passalacqua supplied the *pizzelle* recipe. Everything but the final assembly of this whimsical sandwich can be done ahead of time. Pizzelle irons are available in specialty cookware stores and gourmet shops, or by mail order. Note that the Crème Fraîche must sit for 1 or 2 days.

Gelato di Limone (at right)

Pizzelle

> 4 *eggs*
> 1 *cup sugar*
> 1 *cup vegetable oil*
> 2 *cups plus 2 tablespoons flour*
> 1¼ *teaspoons baking powder*
> ½ *teaspoon salt*
> 1 *teaspoon anise-flavored apéritif*
> 1 *teaspoon grated lemon rind*
> 1 *teaspoon lemon juice*

Strawberry Sauce

> 2 *pints fresh strawberries*
> *Juice of ½ lemon*
> 1 *tablespoon orange-flavored liqueur*
> 2 *tablespoons brown sugar*

Crème Fraîche

> 1 *cup whipping cream, preferably not ultrapasteurized*
> 1 *tablespoon buttermilk*

Cut a Pizzelle in half. Place one half on the bottom of a large dinner plate. Place two small scoops Gelato di Limone on top. Top with other Pizzelle half. Put a dollop of Crème Fraîche on top and a little Strawberry Sauce on the side.

Makes about 1 dozen sandwiches.

Pizzelle Put eggs and sugar in a large bowl and whisk until light. Add oil and whisk well. Sift together flour, baking powder, and salt. Add to egg mixture with liqueur, lemon rind, and lemon juice. Beat just until blended. Bake in a pizzelle iron according to manufacturer's directions. Extra portions may be .cooled and frozen.

Makes about 3 dozen small pizzelle.

Strawberry Sauce Wash, dry, and hull the berries, reserving eight of the largest ones. Put the rest in a processor or blender along with lemon juice, liqueur, and sugar. Process or blend until smooth. Strain through a fine sieve. Cut the reserved berries in thick slices and stir them into the sauce. Chill sauce until ready to serve.

Makes about 2 cups.

Crème Fraîche Combine cream and buttermilk in a clean glass jar with a lid; shake well. Set aside at room temperature until thickened, 24 to 48 hours. (Crème Fraîche will keep, refrigerated, for up to 1 week.)

Makes about 1 cup.

GELATO DI LIMONE
Lemon ice cream

Most Italians buy their ice cream from street vendors, but it is easily made at home with an ice cream freezer. With diced fresh lemon and orange liqueur, this homemade version far outshines commercial products.

> 1 *small lemon*
> 1 *tablespoon honey*
> 1 *tablespoon orange-flavored liqueur*
> ⅓ *cup sugar*
> ¾ *cup half-and-half*
> 1 *vanilla bean*
> *Pinch salt*
> 3 *egg yolks*
> ½ *cup whipping cream*
> ½ *cup Crème Fraîche (at left)*

1. Grate rind from lemon and reserve. Using a small sharp knife, remove all the remaining white pith. Section lemon and cut flesh into ¼-inch dice. In a small bowl combine honey and liqueur. Add diced lemon and let marinate 2 hours at room temperature.

2. Put lemon rind and sugar in a food processor or blender and process or blend until sugar almost begins to melt. Set aside. Put half-and-half in a medium saucepan. Cut vanilla bean in half crosswise, then split one piece in half lengthwise. Scrape seeds from the two split quarters into the half-and-half, then add the split quarter-pods to the half-and-half as well. Save remaining vanilla-bean piece for another use. Bring half-and-half to a simmer over moderate heat, then add sugar-lemon mixture and salt. Whisk well to combine and remove from heat.

3. Whisk yolks in a small bowl; add ½ cup of the hot half-and-half mixture, whisk well, and mix back into the rest of the half-and-half. Return saucepan to low heat and cook, stirring constantly, until mixture reaches 175° F. Do not allow to boil. Remove from heat and strain mixture through a sieve into a stainless steel bowl. Cool; then stir in cream and Crème Fraîche. Chill mixture 2 hours, then stir in marinated diced lemon and freeze in an ice cream machine according to manufacturer's directions. Do not serve ice cream directly from the freezer; let it soften 5 minutes in the refrigerator before serving.

Makes 3 cups, serves 6.

INDEX

127

U.S. MEASURE AND METRIC MEASURE CONVERSION CHART

Formulas for Exact Measures					Rounded Measures for Quick Reference		
	Symbol	When you know:	Multiply by:	To find:			
Mass (Weight)	oz	ounces	28.35	grams	1 oz		= 30 g
	lb	pounds	0.45	kilograms	4 oz		= 115 g
	g	grams	0.035	ounces	8 oz		= 225 g
	kg	kilograms	2.2	pounds	16 oz	= 1 lb	= 450 g
					32 oz	= 2 lb	= 900 g
					36 oz	= 2¼ lb	= 1,000 g (1 kg)
Volume	tsp	teaspoons	5.0	milliliters	¼ tsp	= 1/24 oz	= 1 ml
	tbsp	tablespoons	15.0	milliliters	½ tsp	= 1/12 oz	= 2 ml
	fl oz	fluid ounces	29.57	milliliters	1 tsp	= ⅙ oz	= 5 ml
	c	cups	0.24	liters	1 tbsp	= ½ oz	= 15 ml
	pt	pints	0.47	liters	1 c	= 8 oz	= 250 ml
	qt	quarts	0.95	liters	2 c (1 pt)	= 16 oz	= 500 ml
	gal	gallons	3.785	liters	4 c (1 qt)	= 32 oz	= 1 liter
	ml	milliliters	0.034	fluid ounces	4 qt (1 gal)	= 128 oz	= 3¾ liters
Temperature	°F	Fahrenheit	5/9 (after subtracting 32)	Celsius	32° F		= 0° C
					68° F		= 20° C
	°C	Celsius	9/5 (then add 32)	Fahrenheit	212° F		= 100° C